insideout

insideout

decorating ideas for an outside living space

gilly love

conran
OCTOPUS

For Stephen Harrington, an extraordinary friend

First published in 2000 by
Conran Octopus Limited
2-4 Heron Quays
London E14 4JP

www.conran-octopus.co.uk

ISBN 1 84091 118 2

Commissioning editor: Stuart Cooper
Senior editor: Emma Clegg
Assistant Editor: Lucy Nicholson
Copy editor: Judy Cox
Proofreader: Colette Campbell
Designer: Sue Storey
Picture research: Liz Boyd
Production controller: Sue Bayliss

British Library Cataloguing-in-Publication Data
A catalogue record for this book is available from the British Library

Colour origination by Sang Choy International, Singapore
Printed in China

CONTENTS

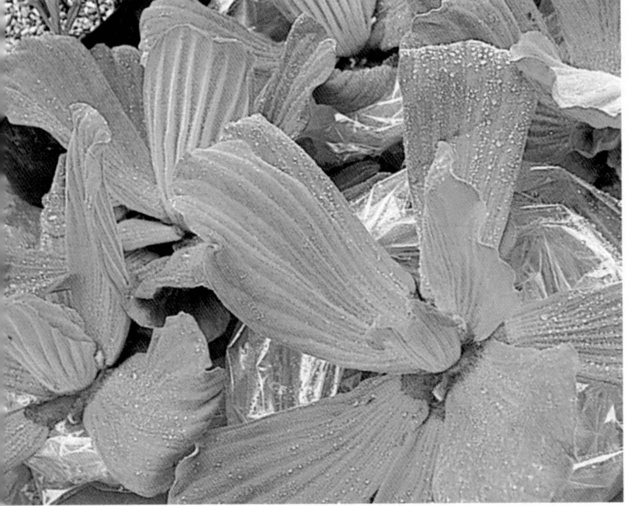

INTRODUCTION

Today's gardens are for people who really want to enjoy their outside space. *Inside Out* is therefore not a traditional gardening manual – it is a book about designing gardens as extensions to the home, with the emphasis on outdoor living rather than horticulture. You do not even need a garden to provide that vital link with the outdoors. A tiny balcony, a roof terrace or a concrete basement all have fantastic potential for providing extra space and spiritual comfort. What really matters is that you create a space where you feel comfortable and where the design works for you and your family, just like every other room in your home.

The contemporary garden can be a place to relax in peace and enjoy the sensory delights that only the natural world can provide, whether this means an area for *al fresco* dining with family and friends or a secluded seat surrounded by aromatic plants. In any outdoor living space, comfort and practicality should be the primary considerations – and simple designs and natural materials will always work best. Focal points such as a beautiful tree can illustrate the changing seasons; or a bed filled with huge sunflowers can recall happy childhood memories; and even the smallest water feature can provide either an exhilarating cascade or a soft, sensuous gurgle. Judicious lighting will create magic, drama and romance, and evenings spent outside can be as fulfilling as days.

If you choose flowers and plants that truly echo your personality you can make this space yours for ever. Use them to enhance the room's design and you will create a style and atmosphere that will change from one season to another – your garden is one room that will never lose its capacity to charm and surprise. Select plants that complement your lifestyle and have the confidence to experiment from season to season. Enthusiastic cooks will delight in growing fresh herbs or even homegrown fruit and vegetables; others will want flowers and foliage to bring indoors. Some people will need a minimalist atmosphere to enjoy stress-free relaxation, while others will find that they prefer a time-consuming space where they can lose themselves for hours, utterly absorbed in growing, tending and watering.

Whatever you choose to do, your outside room will be unique – a special place to refresh your spirits, calm your nerves and feed your soul. *Inside Out* will help you create personal space where you can truly be yourself.

assessing your garden

Designing your own garden is a challenging adventure, an opportunity to discover and appreciate the world around you. The most successful interiors have one element in common – they are designed specifically for the people who live in them. The same good design principles of form and function, planning and detail are essential ingredients for creating gardens that are truly personalized spaces.

LEFT A contemporary interpretation of the potager *or kitchen garden, which was the 1999 theme of the Festival International des Jardins at Chaumont-sur-Loire, France.*

Your connection to the outdoor world may be achieved by means of a garden, a roof terrace, a balcony, or even a window box, but on whatever level it is pitched, this provides a vital link to nature. At a time when the world has few truly wild places remaining, we are becoming very concerned about nature, conservation and ecology, and this has made us appreciate our gardens more than ever before.

Modern gardeners are often not experienced horticulturalists but people who appreciate the sensory satisfaction of enjoying their own outside space. We all need a special place of peace and tranquillity, a private little piece of paradise. If we have no access to the outside world and cannot relish the sights, sounds and smells of the changing seasons, we deny ourselves contact with nature and a real understanding of the need to protect and value our fragile environment. Nearly a decade ago the English garden designer John Brookes wrote: 'The garden is still, as it ever was, a retreat, but it is no longer a retreat from the "awe-fulness" of Nature; rather it is a retreat from the awfulness of the twentieth-century manifestations of Man himself.'

Over the centuries garden design has been subject to great changes of style, and shifts in the way that nature has been perceived and interpreted. Many contemporary gardens are inspired by the concept of the paradise garden, a legacy of the Islamic style where the garden was an enclosed sanctuary filled with the sight and sound of water and shade, a place set apart from the harshness of the desert beyond its walls. Replace the scorching desert with the urban jungle of busy streets and traffic jams, and it is easy to see that we too need an oasis of peace and quiet.

Other historical influences are the gardens of medieval monasteries, which were built around a cloistered quadrangle, imitating the architecture of Roman villas. These enclosed gardens produced medicinal herbs for the infirmaries, and flowers for garlands and festivals. They are the

ancestors of modern herb gardens, where we can also grow fresh organic vegetables in pots and containers.

Contemporary gardens, above all, are an extension of the home, with house and garden intrinsically linked. The garden may be a small terrace or balcony, or a series of interconnected spaces that can be perceived as outside 'rooms'. The key to its success has as much to do with careful planning and design awareness as with horticultural training.

Trees, plants and shrubs are nevertheless an important design element and are vital in creating a mood or emphasizing a particular style. To get ideas, you can visit gardens, read books and seek advice from reputable nurseries.

Left: A sun-baked wall and stone banquette surrounded by aromatic planting provide a place of quiet seclusion. A couple of sheets that are suspended on thin poles look more appropriate in this relaxed setting than a more formal parasol.

Above: Perhaps the most important element of this Mediterranean garden is its breathtaking view. A low wall defines the terrace perimeter, with dense evergreen planting either side, producing an effective windbreak.

A room with a view

Space, proportion and natural light are the most important ingredients of modern living, quite independent of fashion or style. The decision we make when choosing a house or apartment to live in involves practical considerations such as location, cost and size, but the perfect home also needs to engender the right feeling to us.

You can make structural changes to increase the size and improve the function of individual rooms, but it is not possible to change the outlook from windows and, more importantly, the light they receive. Homes without windows would be impossible to live in – we all need natural light for our bodies to function healthily, and sunlight creates a feeling of optimism that lifts our spirits. Rooms with a view command a premium in hotels because your enjoyment of a holiday is dramatically affected if you wake up every morning greeted by a stunning view, as opposed to the sight of a brick wall outside the window. Few of us are lucky enough to have a home surrounded by beautiful countryside but the outlook is always an important consideration.

When buying a house, look out at the views from the windows and observe the type of light they receive. You will probably not have the opportunity to view it in every season, but it is sound advice to walk around the property at different times of day and night. Note where the light comes in and for how long it remains inside and, just as important, outside. Most homes do not face one direction exactly and the quality and quantity of natural light can often be affected by other buildings, walls or trees. The quantity of light may be simple to improve if it is impeded by a vigorous climber or overhanging branches that obscure a window, but you can hardly demolish your next-door-neighbour's house or the five-storey school opposite.

Right: The clean lines of the modern architecture, the wide expanses of glass and a crisp mesh metal panel are all reflected in the still, shallow pool which improves the humidity in this enclosed space.

Below: This perfect solution for a basement dining room, which seamlessly merges into the garden is achieved by using the same colours and materials for both the interior and exterior floors and walls.

Right: Effective shelter and shade are vital when creating an outside room and this verandah basks in the warmth of the sun, while also being shaded from the discomfort of overhead glare. An exterior water source is another essential feature, along with an outside light that clearly illuminates the entrance.

Extending space

If your potential new home is in need of improvement and if finances and planning permission permit, a roof terrace, garden room extension or patio will provide an outside living space. Even replacing a window can make an enormous difference, particularly if it is one that gives access to the outdoors. In older houses the kitchen and basement have often become the central living area, a combined kitchen and dining space that seamlessly spills out into the garden. A dining room that overlooks a garden will be completely transformed by the addition of fully glazed French windows. The light in the room is dramatically improved, whatever the season, and when the weather is warm and the doors are opened the garden or terrace becomes an integral part of the home rather than a separate space. It is a functional juxtaposition of inside and outside space specifically designed for people to live in comfortably all year round.

Choosing a style

The style you choose for your outside space is an entirely personal one; whether you go for fashionable colours, understated simplicity or classical style depends on your individual taste. You could project a fantasy image of how you see yourself, or alternatively a true and honest picture of your character and lifestyle. Fashion and social change have dictated the style of how rooms have been designed and decorated, and then rearranged and altered. It is too early to find a label for the first century of the third millennium, but there is a powerful desire to put aside convention and to shape inside and outside 'rooms' to meet the needs of their owners. Forget the notion that a garden is just a place for plants – plants are an essential element, but not the sole reason for a garden to exist. Consider more carefully the need for an outside room to cook and eat in, a place to work and read, a private area to play and relax in.

Below: A tubular steel pergola is the framework for a temporary canvas canopy that can easily be adjusted according to the sun's position. Low Japanese-style benches follow the shape of the terrace, not impeding the surrounding view.

Glass rooms – the options

One of the most attractive ways of combining living indoors with outside pleasures is to extend your home with a conservatory. Historically, conservatory structures only became viable in the eighteenth century when developments in the manufacture of glass permitted the construction of hothouses and orangeries. These rooms were inspired by a romantic notion of worshipping nature, which began in France and spread very rapidly among the privileged classes of Europe. Conservatories were designed to show off precious and tender plants and flowers to dramatic effect, and to impress and entertain. They exuded pleasure, leisure and conspicuous wealth and were rooms in which house-owners could feel in contact with nature while being protected from the weather. These glass spaces had very little in common with the more functional demands of other rooms in the house.

Traditional conservatories were designed for plants and provided a high level of humidity that was not comfortable for people. However, the concept of the glasshouse has survived several hundred years, to be revived and re-invented to provide a practical living space that integrates harmoniously with existing architecture rather than a superfluous room tacked on to the side of a building. Thanks to modern building techniques and the sophistication of glass technology, it is possible to construct a glass room on any level, facing any aspect and for it to provide a comfortable living environment all year round. To achieve this, meticulous planning and good construction are essential, including double-glazing, toughened safety glass, effective ventilation and security locks on doors and opening windows.

Right: Removing part of a kitchen wall opens up and incorporates space from what would otherwise be a redundant outside corridor. This makes space for a dining area with a glazed ceiling and an open view of the garden beyond.

The shape of the interior of a conservatory can dramatically affect the space available. Bay-shaped designs will limit where you can place furniture, for instance, and although an octagonal room may look attractive it will inevitably prove more difficult to furnish than a simple, regular shape. The direction in which a conservatory faces creates very different demands on the way the room is heated and cooled. North-facing glass rooms require very efficient heating in winter, whereas a south-facing conservatory may be oppressively hot in summer unless its roof is shaded and it is equipped with fully opening doors and windows. These extremes of temperature, that are rarely encountered in other rooms, will either make a conservatory a practical living space or a 'no-go' area for much of the year.

So is a conservatory the right solution? A fully glazed room with sensitive temperature control and high humidity is a paradise for many plants. Conservatories can make even the slowest-growing tropical plants develop to their full potential but they may be more susceptible to insect infestation and require regular spraying with pesticides. For the dedicated plant collector and gardener, a conservatory is ideal; it is the perfect environment to raise seeds, to over-winter tender specimens and to grow exotic plants that flower all year round.

You can still be true to nature and enjoy the comforts of modern living by creating a partially glazed extension in which the plants inside are mere accessories, the garden outside feels more intimate and there is a natural flow from house to garden.

Above: The style and character of the interior furnishings and colours are echoed in the tones and textures of the paving, planting and garden trellis.

Left: From the garden looking back at the conservatory, harmony prevails. As the glazing is restricted to the front elevation and central roof lantern light, the extension remains cool in summer.

Research and planning

Consulting a reputable architect is a wise decision when contemplating major structural changes, and he or she will be able to explain the possibilities and also any restrictions. Construction may involve removing some, if not all, of the rear elevation of a building but widening a doorway or eliminating part of a wall could drastically improve the natural light and space in existing rooms, as well as improving the air flow and ventilation in the extension.

Many successful contemporary garden rooms have glazed roofs with solid walls and, if the ceiling height is raised to construct a lantern roof, this creates a well-proportioned space, filled with natural light and moving shadows that subtly change from season to season. When such rooms are well designed, often combined with a kitchen, they provide an attractive space for living, cooking and eating. A practical kitchen benefits from having a casual dining space that is linked to both the cooking and preparation area and to the garden. Provided it is built to the highest standards of insulation and ventilation, condensation is not a problem and most modern kitchen furniture will not fade even when subjected to direct sunlight.

Below: An enclosed outside space can reflect the atmosphere of its surroundings by using sympathetic colours.

Modern conservatories need to function like any other room in the home, so their decorative scheme calls for an approach that blends the garden with the house. The plain, bright white favoured by the Victorians for their conservatories will not be the most sympathetic colour to choose today. A combination of warm and neutral tones is easier to live with and these colours will blend harmoniously with your exterior masonry.

Terracotta floor tiles used to be a popular traditional choice for flooring but, unless they are well weathered and faded, a large expanse of orange can be difficult to live with and will restrict other decorating decisions. One good way to make a modern extension blend with older architecture is to lay a reclaimed floor, which makes up for the lack of architectural features and provides instant character. The softer, more subtle, neutral hues of limestone, creamy marble or bleached pavers echo contemporary taste for natural-toned carpets and seagrass matting.

A wooden floor, either naturally coloured or stained, will blend perfectly with exterior decking in natural honey-coloured treated pine or a darker and more expensive Western red cedar hardwood. Decking is a practical choice, particularly if you need to raise the outside ground level to match that of the interior, and it is a warm and friendly surface for children and for bare feet, even in winter.

Flooring in a garden room does not need to exactly match its adjoining exterior, but it makes for a more seamless transition if it is of a similar tone. It also makes practical sense to have an area of hard surface between this room and the garden.

Consulting a garden designer

Once you step outside, your design and decorating confidence may begin to falter. Before you make any major decisions, a consultation with a professional garden designer could save both heartache and costly mistakes. An experienced and sensitive designer will be able to interpret your ideas and requirements, and also to present you with ways and means of how to achieve them successfully.

Allay the fear that a professional will take over the project and present you with a colossal invoice. You may decide that all you need is a plan that you can execute yourself within your own timescale. One advantage of employing a competent designer is that he or she will have first-hand experience of good contractors for both hard and soft landscaping, plus knowledge of reputable nurseries. Many garden centres employ their own designers, and although they tend to specify their own plants and products, this is an economical way of starting from scratch. Gardening magazines often offer a postal design service and for a very reasonable fee you can get lots of ideas for your garden without any further obligation.

Left: This rooftop garden in Manhattan was undoubtedly designed to be seen rather than walked upon. The Japanese-inspired landscape of bronze galvanised strips are decoratively infilled with a mat-forming sedum and smooth river stones.

Far left: A half-curtain of sky-blue glass beads frames the entrance to this plant-filled London roof terrace. In summer the datura and lavender fill this tiny space with sweet fragrance.

It can be extremely comforting and reassuring to commission a garden designer at least for an initial site visit. As well as being able to see their portfolio of previous projects, a good indicator of both their skill and imagination, you will receive an evaluation of your space and its aspect, soil, location and climatic implications. Make the most of this visit by preparing a list of questions you want to ask and walk round with them. Help the designer, too, by compiling a selection of pictures that you are inspired by. They could be your own photographs of gardens and landscapes you have seen, or taken from books and magazines, but they will help to give the designer a clear indication of your preferred style and aspirations.

The most successful design schemes, both inside and out, often evolve from a single idea or inspiration. Garden designers generally have a very

definite style of their own and this is why people are drawn to them in the first instance, but when it comes to advising clients, a good designer should concentrate on the needs and personalities of the client rather than trying to impose their own personal taste against yours.

If you do decide to employ a designer to produce a detailed design, you need to have first-hand experience of their approach if you are to build a successful relationship. More input from you will make for a more appropriate scheme. Take note of the questions they ask you as an indication of their professionalism. They should enquire about the lifestyles of the people who will use the outside space. Busy people with demanding jobs may prefer a low-maintenance garden that can be enjoyed especially in the evenings, which may be their only opportunity to appreciate it apart from weekends. Outdoor decking would create a low-maintenance platform for dining and entertaining, and evening scented plants and an attractive lighting scheme would make the most of summer twilight. With a powerful patio heater, which resembles a giant hurricane lamp, you could eat al fresco for almost all the year round.

Small children, or plans to have a family in the near future, will have a significant influence on a design. Avoid ponds or water features that children could topple into, ensure that flooring is soft and warm underfoot, and that any planting is robust and free from thorns or spiky leaves. If you are away from home regularly, you may want to consider fail-safe security arrangements, a timer-controlled irrigation system or drought-friendly trees and shrubs. If you are always away in July, for example, avoid flowers and plants, soft fruit and vegetables that reach their peak then and are at their most demanding. A garden should be designed to suit you without your having to be a slave to your sweet peas and lettuces.

Garden designers will inevitably ask you about your budget. Be prepared and be honest. If you are to create a fully functional outdoor room, you should compare it to designing and building a kitchen from scratch so you need to allocate the level of budget you would set aside for that. The implementation of most garden plans can be spread over a period of months, even years. Most interior designers will agree that, however tight the budget, they will apportion a significant amount of it to the flooring, and the same applies to an outside room. In small spaces, an outside room may only need one flooring material if it is to be in proportion with the rooms of the house.

Space planning is vital when you are preparing the blueprint for a terrace and it has to be big enough to meet the demands you plan for it. As it is adjacent to the house, it is usually the obvious

Above: This slightly elevated view shows how a simple but well-proportioned design is transformed into a pleasing pattern of hard landscaping and structural planting.

Right: Mature trees are integrated into this bold and extrovert garden design. In this way the eye is encouraged to look further than the perimeter wall to the landscape beyond.

place for entertaining, so you have to consider seating, space for a dining table and room to move around it. Electricity and water are other design elements that need consideration before laying a solid floor. Even if your current budget does not allow for artificial lighting, a water feature or an irrigation system, the conduits for power and water can be laid to be connected at a later date. It would be foolish to design an outside room without an exterior tap, for example, and it needs to be thoroughly insulated if there is the remotest chance of frost. The pipework can run up the side of the building or be attached to a boundary wall.

Whether you are engaging a designer or undertaking the project yourself, it costs nothing to take your time when making decisions. Whatever you choose to do will become part of your life for the foreseeable future. We can all afford to make mistakes by trying to grow a plant in the wrong place or in the wrong soil; this kind of error can easily be rectified and, if not, a plant's demise can be put down to the learning process of gardening. Erecting a cheap trellis that falls down in the first strong wind or employing a contractor who lays a paved terrace with no fall, so that it doesn't drain properly after rain, are expensive and irritating experiences, time-consuming and costly to remedy. Good design is just as important as horticultural supremacy so on the first warm and sunny day of the year, when you feel an uncontrollable desire to spend a fortune at the nearest garden centre, stop and think for a minute. Plants and flowers are the finishing touches to an outside room, an essential element but only within the framework of a well-conceived design. They are, however, often the instant gratification you need when work is in progress. A window box brimming with scented hyacinths may raise your spirits when the garden is being excavated and your view is one of cement-mixers and piles of bricks.

Timber decking that is constructed on a series of interconnected levels solves the problem of sloping land, making a smooth visual transition between the house and its woodland surround. The mellow tone of the natural wooden floor is perfectly complemented by the channels of weed-suppressing pebbles and pea shingle from which silky tufts of grasses sprout up like green fountains.

Styles and inspirations

Identifying what you have in terms of site, climate and aspect, and deciding what you want to enjoy within this outside space, are the building blocks to creating an original and personal Eden. Style is completely individual but there are bound to be like-minded people whose ideas and designs you will be inspired by.

Modernist outdoor rooms are an update on minimalist interiors, so if you prefer uncluttered spaces with pared-down detail that engender a sense of calmness and tranquillity, you may be attracted to the 'less is more' influence of Le Corbusier. This controversial architect of the 1920s was a keen advocate of roof terraces and incorporated them as an integral part of many of his municipal housing and private domestic commissions. Experiment with modern, streamlined floors; boundaries created by concrete and decking interspersed with pebbles and pea shingle; extensive use of still water in curved or geometric pools; structural plants in galvanized or shiny metal containers; and low-voltage lighting sunk into the ground or around the edges of water features.

A more eclectic approach would be to adopt influences and ideas gleaned from all over the world. Global travel has given us the opportunity to experience a diverse wealth of art and crafts, architecture and landscapes. Drought-friendly Mediterranean planting on terraced gravel, intimate groves of rustling Japanese bamboo, wind chimes and trickling water suit the ancient philosophy of feng shui, while huge terracotta pots, or *pithoi*, from Crete and giant Burmese water urns can be used to make dramatic garden sculptures. A collection of these elements creates a melting-pot of familiar and foreign, antique and new. A piece of sculpture, the beauty of an existing tree or an irrepressible desire to build an authentic Caribbean *casita* may be the focus for an original design. Turning your garden into a haven for bees and birds, or an organic allotment for fruit and vegetables, is also within the realms of possibility.

If you find yourself short of ideas, get out and visit inspirational gardens, parks, exhibitions, festivals or anywhere where outside space is used creatively. Contemporary makers, painters and sculptors are producing installations, furniture and ornamental features that represent refreshing new views of garden-making. There is a wealth of inspiration once you start looking, and if it is the cutting edge of innovative garden design you crave, then the place to go is the Festival International des Jardins at the Château de Chaumont-sur-Loire in France, held every year between June and October. Since 1992, part of the park of Chaumont has been dedicated to the garden of the twenty-first century. Jacques Wirtz, the acclaimed Belgian designer, has devised a pattern of 30 individual spaces, each approximately 250m (275yd) square and enclosed by beech hedges, and landscape designers and artists from all over the world are invited to create a garden on a particular theme, which changes each year. Some of these gardens have been so successful and popular with visitors they have been kept and are meticulously maintained.

One garden that has inspired me more than any other is the extraordinary space created by the late Derek Jarman, painter, theatre designer, film-maker and passionate gardener from childhood. His garden surrounds a wooden fisherman's cottage on the shingle at Dungeness in Kent, a bleak place on a triangular stretch of land bordered by the sea on two sides. The surrounding landscape is gorse and pebbles, with the looming sight of a nuclear power station in the distance.

In the inhospitable climate of salty winds and pervading sea mists, and from 1986 until his death in 1994, Jarman produced a personal landscape without visible boundaries, combining the indigenous plants of the area with traditional seaside plants such as angelica, lavender, rosemary, santolina and erysimum. Stones and pebbles gathered from the shoreline, sorted by colour and graded by size, create curved patterns, their contours emphasized by longer flint stones. Wigwams of

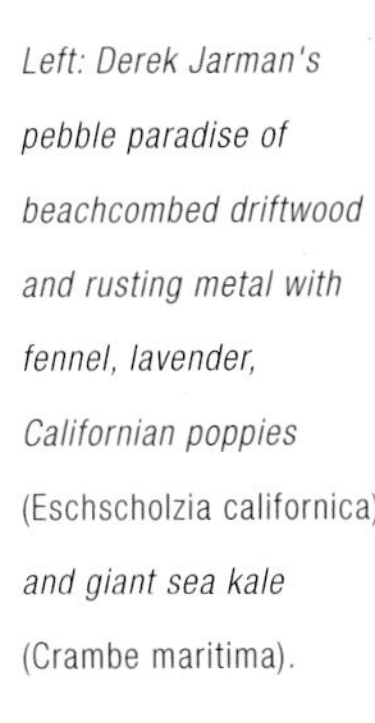

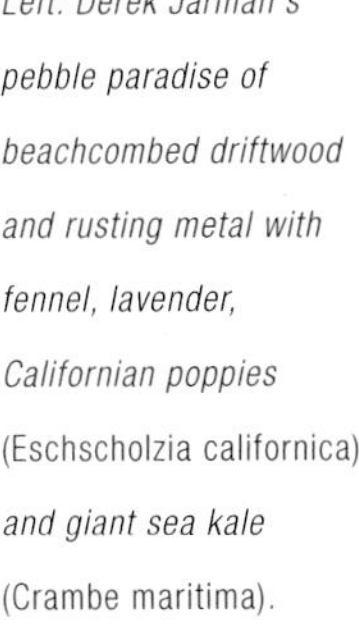

Left: Derek Jarman's pebble paradise of beachcombed driftwood and rusting metal with fennel, lavender, Californian poppies (Eschscholzia californica) *and giant sea kale* (Crambe maritima).

Below: More inspiration from the Chaumont garden festival, with jets and fountains of water tumbling over rocks and boulders that are studded with curved patterns of small stones and pebbles.

Left: Wit and humour have a place in the garden as is shown by this ingenious water display, featured as part of the annual Festival International des Jardins at the Château de Chaumont-sur-Loire.

beachcombed sticks, originally constructed to protect gorse cuttings from rabbits, and sea-weathered poles and planks used to support tender stems from the wind inspired a collection of natural sculptures that have survived the harshest winter winds. Using reclaimed railway sleepers, Jarman constructed two raised beds, filled with imported soil, for growing herbs and vegetables. These beds also provided protection for a beehive, whose occupants feasted happily on the maritime flowers.

This wondrous place has the atmosphere of a Japanese meditational garden, combined with elements often found in English cottage gardens, and deliberately emphasizes the fragile relationship between a manmade and a natural environment. It also demonstrates how gardening presents a glorious opportunity to lose yourself and discover the pleasures of the outside world.

Colour palette

Creating a harmonious balance of texture, form and tone in an outside space relies on a sensitive choice of colour. This can dramatically or subtly affect the mood and the ambience of the area. Pavings, walls, fences, ornaments and furniture all contribute to the colour in a garden.

Exterior paint and woodstain ranges, specially made to weather sun, rain and frost, provide gardeners with a useful tool for creating permanent colour. Introduced in this way, colour may unify a garden design, add small touches of sharp contrast or neutralise harsh surfaces. Although synthetic colours change endlessly according to the seasons, such permanent tones applied to walls and floors require more careful planning than the more temporary accessories such as awnings or cushions.

Storyboard

Before making any decorating decision, interior designers generally compile a storyboard of colours and textures in roughly the proportion they are likely to be used. They will often spot test a small area with a potential colour before painting an entire room. Wood can be treated in the same way, but when staining exterior timbers ensure that you know whether it is softwood or hardwood as the finished results can be quite different in tone.

Many wood finishes combine a stain and varnish that flexes with the wood to prevent cracking or peeling. Sheds, trellis and fences made from rough sawn timber require a formula combined with preservative to prevent rot and inhibit mould growth. The advantage of choosing a woodstain is that it absorbs into the timber and allows the natural grain and character of the timber to show through.

floors & walls

The two most important elements of any outside space are the floors and walls. Ground surfaces and boundaries must be well considered, as their size and proportion will define an area. They must be constructed with good solid foundations if they are to withstand inevitable changes in the ambient climate. These two features should complement each other and need to be planned together for the most successful results.

LEFT Shades of red are powerful and eye-catching and because of their 'advancing' quality can make spaces appear smaller. Green is the complementary colour to red and throws these stems into sharp contrast.

The ground, or floor, surface is the first element to consider when designing an outside space. Interior and garden designers always start with a basic floor plan, then divide the space and allocate specific areas to meet their clients' requirements.

In your garden you may want to create a terrace adjacent to the house, a raised bed for herbs, space for a shed, tall shrubs to screen an ugly building or a water feature. Draw a plan of the space on graph paper using a scale of 1:10, where each 1cm (½in) square represents 1m (3ft 3in), or a scale of 1:5 where a 1cm (½in) square represents 50cm (20in). Mark all the existing elements accurately and pencil in the proposed new features. Planning both interiors and gardens is similar to assembling a mosaic in which everything is fitted together to form a harmonious living pattern. If you cut out pieces of paper scaled to the size of the new features, you can move them around your plan as you would furniture in a room. A floor plan will influence where and how to co-ordinate existing and new features, and allocating them space on paper will help you to determine the surface they require and how they are linked together.

Choosing a floor surface

The surface material for an outside space can be compared to the icing on a cake, but good quality and appropriate foundations are crucial. Try to be practical and realistic. You may fantasize about turning the whole space into a wildflower meadow, a wonderfully romantic project – but this will not be an option if you want a low-maintenance space. To turn an urban garden into a country paradise could involve removing all the topsoil and replacing it with grit, stones and sand, all well dug in, then waiting several years to achieve your dream. Unless you have a huge area to play with, it is more pragmatic

Right: A polished wooden floor merges with the timber decking that accommodates a series of mature trees. This is a successful way to create a seamless link between the interior and its connecting outside space.

to design a space for living that you can enjoy for the majority of the year and to minimize the stress involved in creating it.

Any outside floor should be well constructed if it is to be hard wearing and able to withstand changes in temperature. If it is to be laid on a balcony or roof, it needs to be watertight. The floor may also need to incorporate a drainage system, power cables for irrigation systems and lighting, and in garden rooms it could include underfloor heating.

The range of outside temperatures should influence your choice. In particular, roof terraces subjected to months of hot sun require a surface that will maintain a reasonably cool temperature, otherwise walking around with bare feet will be impossible. One of the joys of stepping outside is to be able to kick off your shoes and feel the fresh air. Timber decking, one of the favourite surfaces in America, is now becoming popular all over Europe. Like any wooden floor, a deck must be made of a suitable timber and laid perfectly flat. It can be constructed like a false floor to make an outside space on the same level as the interior floor; unlike other flooring materials, water will drain between the planks. As well as creating a transition between house and garden, a deck will cover sloping or uneven ground and can conceal an old, worn-out patio. If there is a considerable drop between the interior and exterior, a raised deck will provide useful storage space underneath. There is a choice of suitable timbers: Western red cedar and iroko are more expensive than the American preference, Southern yellow pine, which is incredibly strong and environmentally sound. Reputable suppliers provide pressure-treated and re-dried timber that is resistant to rot and insect decay. It can be stained or left to weather naturally to a soft driftwood grey, which is compatible with brick, slate and stone.

In hot spots such as roof terraces and balconies, avoid a bright, white floor surface as the intense light will reflect up into your eyes and make relaxing and reading uncomfortable. Softer, neutral colours such as cream, taupe and buff blend easily with brick and stone, and with soft landscaping. On a patio, balcony or roof terrace, it looks very effective to echo the colour of the interior floor with the adjoining exterior.

Unless the ground is liable to extreme heat, solid floors of concrete, stone slabs or pavers are the most practical adjacent to a building. The surfaces of halls and entrances always receive more wear than those in bedrooms, so just as you would choose a heavy-duty carpet or flooring on these areas, use hard wearing surfaces for outside entrances and exits. Unlike a timber deck which can be laid completely flat next to a building because water drains between the planks, a solid floor requires a slope or a 'fall' away from the house with a minimum gradient of 1:100 to prevent water puddling. In situ concrete, which is cast on site, can look very effective when it is laid to a professional standard and dyes or coloured gravel can be added to make it look more interesting.

Above: This garden is infused with the soft, warm light of an evening sunset. The sheltering wall is painted in a dusky terracotta and then decorated with a Moorish-style design that echoes the shapes of the surrounding trees.

Above: Within a large garden it may be desirable to include an expanse of lawn, which can then be combined with other surfaces. This raised paved area is defined by hedging and then divided with the soft landscaping by means of two broad steps.

Lawn versus gravel

A frequent dilemma facing the owners of many small gardens is the lawn. If you inherit a small grassy space, should you keep it? Remember that even a tiny piece of turf needs mowing, watering, feeding and de-mossing to keep it in good health. Then there is the equipment and where to store it. If you must have a lawn, give it a well-defined shape – formal, straight edges are more contemporary than undulating curves, although the latter provide areas for planting flowers and shrubs. It is well worth laying a mowing edge of bricks or paving that allows the lawnmower to run easily over the top. This edge gives the lawn good definition, protects plants in the borders and avoids having to hand-cut the grass edges. Simple or intricate patterns based on circles or squares can be created with stone or concrete paving stones or bricks. Fill in the sections with small stones or gravel, or even plant them with neatly trimmed grass. A geometric chequerboard pattern of bricks filled in with gravel or planted with herbs such as chamomile (*Chamaemelum nobile Treneaguei*), Corsican mint (*Mentha requienni*) or creeping thyme (*Thymus serpyllum*) will release an aromatic scent when crushed underfoot.

Areas of gravel contained by brick or stone borders give a degree of flexibility to a garden. Gravel is fast replacing the urban lawn in popularity as a low-maintenance surface, which can include planting 'pockets' for Mediterranean perennials that tolerate neglect provided they are given a sunny spot and good drainage. Beth Chatto's inspirational gravel garden, created on a dry site previously used as a car park, is living proof that lavender, rosemary, santolina, rue and sage will flourish in these arid conditions. All these plants are strongly scented because the aromatic oils in their leaves help to conserve moisture and protect them from drought. In shady positions, gravel provides dry walkways between moisture-loving ferns and hostas.

Raised beds add character to a space and provide the equivalent of a huge container filled with the soil of your choice and planted accordingly. A raised bed increases the temperature of the soil, which does make it drier, but also protects vulnerable plants from the worst frost. Tall evergreen shrubs will provide year-round shade, shelter and privacy or, alternatively, the bed can be planted with fast-growing perennials such as *Verbena bonariensis* or sweet fennel (*Foeniculum vulgare*). Both of these plants grow to a height of 2m (6½ft) and create a semi-transparent screen that will visually divide one part of the garden from another. Alternatively you could create the same effect with annual climbers trained on ornamental supports such as bamboo wigwams, metal, willow or hazel obelisks. Most of the old-fashioned sweet peas (*Lathyrus odorata*) are sweetly perfumed and will provide flowers for cutting all through the summer, and runner beans (*Phaseolus coccineus*) will create lush foliage and pretty flowers followed by a crop of fresh beans at the end of the summer.

Below: Gravel, stones and pebbles make an excellent mulch, helping to retain precious water and suppressing the growth of unwanted plants, and also making weeding unnecessary.

Above: Insets such as pebbles and inset tiles add vibrant colour and texture. The bases of recycled bottles were pressed into a bed of cement while it was still soft to create a blue reflective surface that is both cool and pleasant underfoot.

Creating different levels

You can add a further dimension to your floor plan by including one or more changes of level. A sloping site may almost demand re-planning in order to make it more people-friendly. A continuous steep slope can be terraced rather like the hills in Umbria, Italy, or those in southern France, where flat steps are cut into the mountainside for planting vines and olive trees. Low, broad terraces defined by low retaining walls and linked by steps paved in complementary materials will transform what may have been previously considered a 'difficult' site. Cultivation on these flat plateaux is much easier and can even include a paved or gravelled area for sitting and entertaining.

Even one change of level can transform an otherwise rather dreary space. A paved terrace in front of a house can be enclosed and sheltered by building a raised bed around its boundaries, linked to another part of the garden by a series of steps.

*Above: A path of broken terracotta pots adjoins a fragrant bank of lavender (*Lavandula x intermedia abrialii*). The pots are filled with purple Heliotrope (*Heliotropium 'Marine'*), white* Lantana camara *and* Helichrysum italicum.

Real and virtual walls

Room dividers such as open bookcases and shelving systems are used very effectively in studio apartments and loft spaces to designate one area from another, and the same technique can be applied outside with decorative trellis, panels of transparent glass bricks, arches and pergolas. Horizontal and vertical surfaces are intrinsically linked in interior design, and they need to be considered together outdoors as well.

A wall, fence or boundary should always be chosen on its own merits and should look attractive without the embellishment of climbers or other planting. Foliage and flowers will soften the contours but they cannot replace quality materials and good construction. A boundary may need to be of a height and material to keep out unwanted intruders, or to create privacy, shelter or shade. The most effective way to create an impenetrable wall is to plant evergreen berberis (*Berberidaceae*) or pyracantha (*Rosaceae*), both of which have virtually invisible but vicious thorns. A chainlink fence between posts secured in concrete bases will economically and effectively define a boundary, and can be concealed in a couple of years with a wildlife hedgerow of bird, bee and butterfly favourites such as elderberry (*Sambucus nigra*), butterfly bush (*Buddleja davidii*) and common hawthorn (*Crataegus monogyna*). Formal hedges of box (*Buxus sempervirens*), hornbeam (*Carpinus betulus*) and yew (*Taxus baccata*) are enjoying a revival, largely because electrically powered hedge-trimmers achieve in minutes what once took hours to cut by hand. To look their best, formal hedges need to be clipped in a slight taper, with the bottom wider than the top to allow air to circulate freely and

so that light can reach all the branches. Less formal hedges of pruned lavender (*Lavandula*), rosemary (*Rosemarinus*) or the taller hazel (*Corylus avellana*) are also good 'room dividers', separating one part of the garden from another. The rose *Rosa rugosa* makes an excellent fast-growing hedge with masses of small bristly thorns, heavily scented deep pink or white flowers, and large autumnal hips which make the best rose-hip syrup.

A new brick wall or fence may require some interesting texture or sympathetic colouring to blend it into its surroundings. An espaliered fruit tree grown against a brick or rendered south- or west-facing wall takes up little space and will thrive in these warm and sheltered positions. Ready-trained trees can be bought from specialist nurseries and, like conventional fruit trees, burst into pretty white blossom in spring, followed by lush foliage and fruit in late summer. Even in winter, when the branches are bare, their shape forms a beautiful living sculpture. Espaliers need regular feeding and careful pruning twice a year, but they are an ideal way to grow fruit trees in a small space.

Left: Painted in subtle shades of blue, two cement-rendered partition walls divide this garden and frame the view of a contemporary water feature. The wall-mounted pot overspills with water, which then trickles softly into the pond below.

Left: A slatted timber wall painted in deep terracotta contrasts with the green foliage of an espaliered fruit tree and a cream picture frame to make a simple but effective focal point.

Below: Wall and ground merge together and interest is created by providing deliberate planting pockets for the contrast of spiky yucca and rosette-forming sempervivum.

Paint effects

Some walls and fences are much improved by paint or woodstain. Rendered walls present a perfect surface for painting but it is important to use a product with a permeable surface; this allows any moisture trapped in the wall to escape, while still protecting the surface. You can create layers of colour by adding painted wooden trellis in a contrasting shade or silvery wire panels. Woodstains are not just limited to timber tones but are available in a rainbow of colours. Many contain a preservative and increase the longevity of the timber, as well as softening the often harsh rusty tones of new fencing. Different timbers will take up colour to varying degrees so it is a good idea to test a small section, let it dry and then inspect the colour before staining an entire fence. If you cannot immediately find the ideal colour, try mixing two or three until you achieve the desired effect.

The walls of a dark basement area can benefit considerably from being painted a soft white or pale neutral tone. Panels of wooden or metal trellis will provide visual interest, either left bare or used to support shade-tolerant climbers. If the basement is sheltered and frost-free, there are numerous tropical plants (more commonly sold as houseplants) that tolerate a warm and shady outside habitat. Another possibility is to securely attach shelves to the walls with metal brackets, and to grow pots of trailing plants such as ivies or cascading ferns. In the tiny courtyards and patios of Andalucia in Spain, vertical surfaces are crammed with pots slotted into metal rings fixed to walls, or hung from guttering or pipes. In this fiercely hot climate the predominant plant is *pelargonium*, which thrives in a minimum of poor soil and flowers profusely for most of the year. Wholesale copying of this style is only really successful if you can provide the same vibrant Spanish sunlight and brilliant blue skies, but the principle of covering your patio wall with hundreds of pots can be stunning. Stick to one colour for the pots and be prepared to spend hours watering, especially if you decide to clad the wall of a roof terrace in this manner.

Right: A wall painted blue provides the foundation for the trellis supporting wisteria on this sunny terrace. Indian saris are suspended between the trellis and the adjoining house to make a colourful shady canopy .

Above: A curved transparent panel extending up from the brick wall creates distorted and abstract reflections of the trees and plants in the foreground.

Right: A wall of multi-layered foliage provides a tiny timber-decked back yard with shade and privacy. Within the fronds of the ground cover ferns are the luminous white flowers of impatiens walleriana.

High-rise walls

The climate on a roof or balcony is different to that on the ground. Summers feel hotter and winter frosts rarely affect these lofty heights, but all-year-round wind can dry out pots, cause leaf-burn to foliage and create an uncomfortable environment for people. Rooftop walls need to filter the power of the wind rather than trying to block it entirely, which causes turbulence. Sturdy trellis performs the job perfectly and is available as pre-formed panels, or as custom-built fences of stout bamboo canes or lightweight metal mesh.

Wattle fencing, made from woven willow branches, is a traditional method for creating solid-looking but wind-permeable walls. A bamboo pole screen will also provide an attractive framework, in front of which climbing plants can be grown in containers. A further filter can be improvised out of

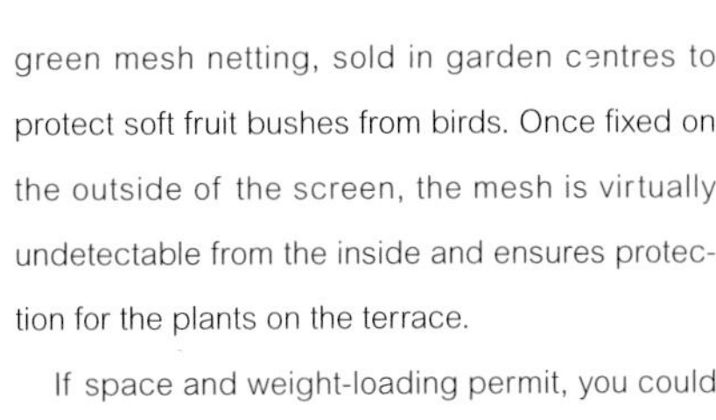

green mesh netting, sold in garden centres to protect soft fruit bushes from birds. Once fixed on the outside of the screen, the mesh is virtually undetectable from the inside and ensures protection for the plants on the terrace.

If space and weight-loading permit, you could grow a completely natural windbreak by creating a hedge of conifer. The dwarf cultivars of Western red cedar (*Thuja plicata*) can easily be controlled by annual clipping, and the leaves and small branches release a wonderful pineapple-like aroma when crushed. On urban rooftops where a terrace is protected by the close proximity of taller buildings, a wall of gently rustling bamboo will provide shelter, shade and privacy.

Above: Texture can add vital interest to repetitive vertical surfaces. This is clearly demonstrated with these bleached wooden poles which are combined with a dense screen of rough twigs that are woven together with fine wire.

PAINTED BRICK WALL

For the reluctant gardener, paint is a very effective way to introduce colour in an outside space. Wooden furniture, fencing, trellis, plant stands and containers can all be painted to harmonize or contrast with their surroundings. Blue is particularly successful with natural greens, enhancing the colour of foliage rather than competing with it. Choose the luminous bold shades found in Mediterranean and Caribbean climates, or the cooler tones used in northern countries where the light is softer.

Water-based masonry paint is available in ready mixed colours, which will provide years of protection. Further colours can be mixed by specialist paint suppliers. If the wall is still powdery after cleaning with a stiff brush it may need a coat of stabilizing solution to seal the surface before painting.

If you are decorating a large wall, it is wise to paint a small area with a tester pot of paint and to observe the result at different times of the day before painting the rest.

MATERIALS AND EQUIPMENT

- plastic dust cover
- wire brush
- large nylon polyester decorator's paintbrush
- deep blue water-based masonry paint
- plastic or rubber lizards
- waterproof adhesive
- small pot of metallic-finish car touch-up paint (optional)
- small artist's paintbrush (optional)
- mussel shells, washed and well scrubbed

1 Protect the ground at the base of the wall with a plastic dust cover. Remove loose dirt or flaking paint with a wire brush. Do not worry about gaps between the bricks as these will be filled with paint and an uneven texture is expected on an exterior wall.

2 A nylon polyester paintbrush gives the best results with water-based paints. Apply the paint generously, filling all the gaps and holes. Leave to dry completely.

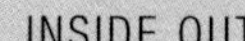

Left: Plastic or rubber lizards such as these can be found at most toy shops.

3 Attach the lizards to the wall with waterproof adhesive, so that they appear to be running up it. If the lizards' skin colouring is too crude, alter it with car touch-up paint, using a small paintbrush.

4 Finally, apply a thick mulch of mussel shells to cover the bare earth at the foot of the wall with a layer of darker blue.

SLATE WITH TIMBER STEPPING STONES

This design was inspired by the peaceful serenity of Japanese gravel gardens. The wooden blocks appear to float on a sea of slate that links a small courtyard to a raised garden beyond. The contrast of colour and texture is pleasing, and this is an ideal way to cover pre-cast concrete paving. One of the attractions of slate is that it changes colour from gleaming dark grey when wet to a pale, light-reflective tone when dry. The slate acts like a mulch and rainwater will soak through the stones and drain away, so fit any outside drain with a grill, using a mesh fine enough to prevent any stones from causing a blockage.

The wooden blocks are free-standing, so they must be heavy enough to walk on safely. Arranged in a path, they lead the eye to discover the more secluded part of the garden beyond. Even small gardens can be divided into distinct spaces, each with its own character.

1 For this path, the timber blocks for the stepping stones were made from three decking planks cut and screwed at right angles to two other planks. Place the stepping stones in position and then surround them with a shallow mulch of slate Paddlestones (see page 139 for supplier).

Left: The lower part of each wooden block should be surrounded by slate, to create a natural effect.

MATERIALS AND TOOLS

- pre-treated timber blocks, each 24cm (9½in) square and 6cm (2½in) deep
- 10–15cm (4–6in) slate Paddlestones (produced industrially in tumbling machines)
- large clam shells

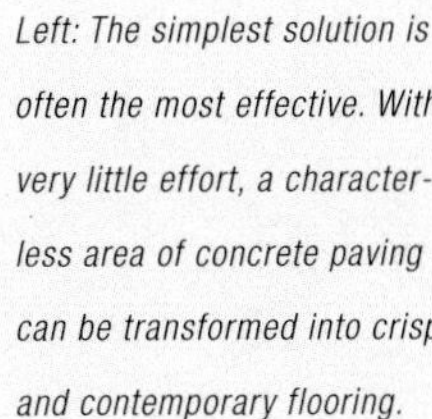
Left: The simplest solution is often the most effective. With very little effort, a characterless area of concrete paving can be transformed into crisp and contemporary flooring.

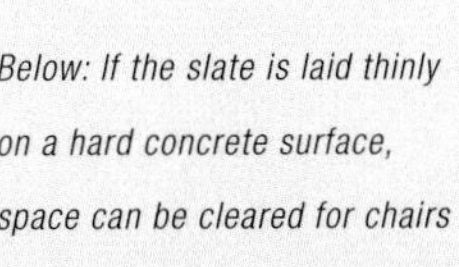
Below: If the slate is laid thinly on a hard concrete surface, space can be cleared for chairs and tables to stand quite safely.

2 As a relief to the formal, horizontal line of the path, you may want to add some rounded shapes. Here, four terracotta pots, planted with round box shapes, are defined with circles of clam shells.

VARIATION

Even pre-treated timber can be coloured using an exterior woodstain. Choose a colour to complement the foliage and contrast with the grey slate.

furniture & furnishings

Relaxation is often one of the main attractions of a garden – it should be a place where you can enjoy the fresh air in peace and privacy. When choosing furniture and furnishings for an outside space, you might like to include a comfortable bench, nestling between aromatic shrubs chosen for their evening scent, or a generous-sized table where you can sit and enjoy a summer lunch with family and friends. Comfort and practicality are key elements here. And remember that simple designs and natural materials will complement any setting.

LEFT The elegantly shaped and perfectly proportioned metal chairs shown here have an eye-catching and sculptural quality. They also serve a dual practical purpose – either for sitting on or for displaying plants.

Above: Built into the walls of a sheltered balcony, this versatile cushioned banquette is long enough to lie on. With the addition of a low table it would also provide a dining space for two or three people.

However you have designed your garden, there will be times when all you really want to do is just sit out there and relax. This is when you discover if you have created a place for people, or a showcase for plants and objects.

Finding the right position for a 'sitting room' contributes considerably to outdoor comfort, so at the preliminary stage mark areas on your plan that are warm and sheltered, ideally offering privacy and with a pleasing outlook.

All the senses must be satisfied in order to achieve a state of complete relaxation. The pleasure of smell is very important out of doors – fresh air has a fantastic scent of its own that can be enhanced by aromatic herbs such as rosemary and lavender, or sweetly perfumed jasmine and roses. Scented flowers create a wonderfully relaxing ambience, particularly in the evening when their fragrance is more intense. An attractive view of green plants and flowers appeals to our sense of sight, and the sound of water and birdsong is very soothing to our ears. Even hard surfaces of stone or metal can be covered with fat, squashy cushions to make them comfortable.

Al fresco dining

Sensitive positioning is as important as your choice of furniture. A raised brick flowerbed can be designed to incorporate a bench seat with the dimensions of a generous sofa, surrounded by scented flowers and shrubs. Constructed along one side of a paved patio, this should be long enough to lie on or to provide seating for three or four people with the support of a well-padded seat and back cushions. Add a rectangular table and free-standing chairs and you can easily accommodate

eight or nine people. This dining area needs at least 3sq.metres (3½sq.yards) of floor space to give freedom of movement and easy access. If this is impossible, you could have a free-standing bench instead of chairs, ideally placed against a wall so that diners have back support. Some outdoor chairs are very lightweight, in which case the ground underneath them needs to be perfectly flat or they will always have an irritating wobble when you sit on them. However, lightweight portable chairs are space-saving as they fold flat or stack neatly.

Where a terrace is adjacent to the kitchen or dining room and on the same level, a dining table with lockable castors could double up for both inside and outside. A weatherproof table that can be left permanently outside may provide a useful place for planted containers, especially in the winter when it is unlikely to be used for dining. A table is also the ideal height for a potting bench. Stone mosaic table tops in vibrant glazed patterns look decorative on a paved terrace, while an unglazed, muted design would blend into the hard landscaping. Marble, limestone and slate make elegant, hard-wearing table tops that withstand any degree of heat or cold from the natural elements and require little maintenance. These materials are perfect for dining as they are unaffected by squashed fruit or spilt salad dressing.

Left: Delicate detailing makes this metal bench as much a decorative object as a practical seat. Its removable cushions blend with the sunbaked colours of this Mediterranean courtyard.

Materials matter

One of the pleasures of al fresco eating is being oblivious of time passing, and this can be achieved only if the seating is comfortable and the dining space sheltered. An outside temperature that seems ideal when you are walking around or working can feel distinctly chilly if you are sitting still. Similarly, oppressively hot sun becomes pleasantly warm when it is filtered or partially blocked. A building or tree canopy may already create shade in your outdoor space, but if not, you can construct an artificial ceiling by rigging up a simple canvas canopy, supported by sturdy wooden or metal poles secured in concrete blocks or directly into the ground. Many outdoor tables have a central hole for a parasol secured with a weighted base. A more elaborate idea is a tubular steel or galvanized metal structure built over and above a permanent seat, which can be transformed into a leafy arbour with roses, clematis or other quick-growing climbers. Alternatively, canvas panels can be tied to the structure to create a temporary shelter from wind and sun. On a small patio or terrace surrounded by solid walls, you may be able to fix metal hooks from which to run metal wires like a curtain track and from these you can attach lengths of canvas or cheaper calico with metal clips.

On an upper terrace or roof garden, extra protection may be required to compensate for the more exposed position. The strongest part of a roof is around its perimeter and here you can construct timber seating, combined with planters and protected by a screen of trellis or another semi-permeable 'wall'. Garden storage can be incorporated under the seat for pots and tools, barbecue charcoal and bags of compost. The base could also be designed to be removed entirely or hinged to a frame. This type of seating is permanent

Below: These concrete benches make permanent and maintenance-free seating. They are subtly decorated with inlaid ceramic tiles – the design echoes the same random pattern of the brick floor.

tile, ranging from simply styled French café chairs and tables to more intricately patterned Victorian-style wrought iron benches. The disadvantage of wrought iron is the cost, particularly for original designs, and also the weight. One advantage of lightweight chairs is that they can be shifted to follow the sun and quickly brought inside if the weather changes.

Many interior furniture designs have evolved for outside use, but have migrated back indoors in response to the need for lightweight folding chairs in small homes and studios. In interiors where storage space is limited, some furniture can be used both inside and outside. Flat-folding canvas and wooden director's chairs with removable seats and backs are comfortable as well as appropriate to the setting. With different sets of canvas covers, these chairs can be adapted to match any colour scheme and because they fold flat, are easily transportable.

Below: These crisp white painted metal French café chairs and simple folding table are classic designs for indoor and out. They stack flat and such furniture is ideal for smaller homes where space for storage is at a premium.

Above: Subtly concealed from obvious view and surrounded by a wall-trained fig and a towering Agapanthus *'Snowy owl', this is a perfect place for a time of quiet seclusion in the soft evening light.*

and therefore needs to be weatherproof. In the past, teak was one of the most popular timbers for outdoor seating but public awareness of the destruction of tropical rainforests has put pressure on manufacturers to find other hardwoods such as English oak, Swedish redwood and timbers harvested from estates with responsible re-planting schemes. Much of this wood is 'tanalized', meaning that it has been impregnated under pressure with tanalith oxide preservative. This treatment protects the wood from any form of degradation, including wet or dry rot, woodworm and other insects, but also offers a surface that can be oiled, stained or painted. Softwoods such as pine are much cheaper, but outdoor furniture made from these timbers may need a fresh coat of wood preservative each year to prevent rotting.

Metal will also succumb to the weathering effects of sun and rain. Distressed surfaces can be attractive, but the hinges of metal tables and chairs should be protected from rusting and oiled regularly to keep them in good working order. Painted metal furniture is immensely functional and versa-

Total relaxation

Many outdoor chairs are perfect for sitting at a table, but a more comfortable, reclining chair is needed for serious relaxation. There are scores of designs developed from the original 'steamer' chairs, created for luxury cruise ships. Rows of these reclining wooden seats with adjustable, elongated leg rests were provided for passengers to enjoy the view of the ocean and breathe the clean, salty air. Passengers used them in all weathers, muffled in warm blankets in winter or shaded by individual parasols in summer. It is still a glorious way to relax. Many contemporary designs are made from hollow metal tube frames with plastic or metal mesh covers. These new versions of the steamer chair are ergonomically designed to be lightweight and easy to carry. Looks are only one consideration, so apply the same comfort requirements as you would when choosing a bed. You need to be able to stretch out totally and to feel supported in the middle of your back.

Perhaps the cheapest and most popular version of the lounger is the good old-fashioned deckchair, whose simple design can still be seen on beaches and in parks all over the world. It is still immensely practical for small outside spaces and newer models are designed so the canvas seat is easy to remove, to be stored somewhere clean and dry when not in use. The deckchair also has the curious ability to look at home in any outdoor setting, be it a formal traditional garden or an ultra-modern terrace. The original versions have a wooden frame but there are now modern designs made of lightweight tubular aluminium frames covered with tough woven synthetic fabrics, and some have a rocking mechanism. The modern 'butterfly' chair consists of a canvas bucket-shaped seat slung on to a wire frame, which folds into a neat bundle; the covers can be removed for storage and the occasional machine wash. In a minimalist outside space, with restrained planting and large areas of concrete or stone, these chairs, judiciously placed, have a pleasing sculptural appearance.

Left: In traditional gardens it is the flowers and plants that introduce colour to the overall design. However in this contemporary outside room, the trees are used for their sculptural quality and it is the lemon and orange canvas butterfly chairs that exude vibrant colour and contrast invitingly with the deep purple perimeter wall.

Above: Gerrit Rietveld designed his celebrated red-blue chair in 1917. His design is now often used as a blueprint by furniture makers, illustrated by this contemporary and more simplified version.

Modern classics

The updated versions of café-style tables and chairs that have replaced slatted wooden furniture are often coated in a hard-wearing, water-resistant resin, subtly coloured in contemporary colours such as aqua, pistachio and lime. Even classically styled metal or wooden benches can be adapted to suit modern surroundings. The designer and architect Sir Edwin Lutyens created elegant furniture for many of the famous gardens he designed in collaboration with Gertrude Jekyll, and with its perfect proportions, it still has a place in today's outdoor spaces.

Natural wood furniture blends with foliage and flowers, but painted or stained a bright cobalt blue or deep Etruscan red it becomes a strong focal point, particularly in the winter garden when there is no other colour. Sympathetic colours can also be applied to other wooden structures such as trellis and planters. One idea is to link the furniture with the detailing of the trellis by repeating the same chinoiserie or lattice pattern on the seat backs.

Less conventional furniture can be instantly created with a wide, splinter-free plank spanned across two logs or piles of bricks. Positioned against a sheltered, east-facing wall, this is the perfect place to enjoy early morning sunshine. For resting at the end of a summer day, nothing beats a hammock. There are modern designs with swing seats on frames, but the simplest version is canvas or a similar fabric sling-tied at two points with rope. Strong supports are, of course, essential and this could be by means of metal hooks driven into brick walls or, more traditionally, rope firmly secured around the trunks of mature, healthy trees.

Above: In rural areas where coppiced wood is cheap and plentiful, rustic designs require only the most rudimentary skills to create practical furniture that blends with other natural materials.

Left: Steamer chairs, reclining wooden seats with adjustable leg rests, once graced the decks of luxury liners. Here, they look equally at home on this timber-decked roof terrace.

CHAIR COVERS

Café-style chairs are very popular as they are lightweight, can be stored flat and, being constructed from metal and wood, are reasonably weatherproof. To make them more comfortable, add simple seat covers filled with foam cushions and slip-over back covers containing a thin layer of foam padding. Use the same fabric in various colours to make a co-ordinated set of mix-and-match covers.

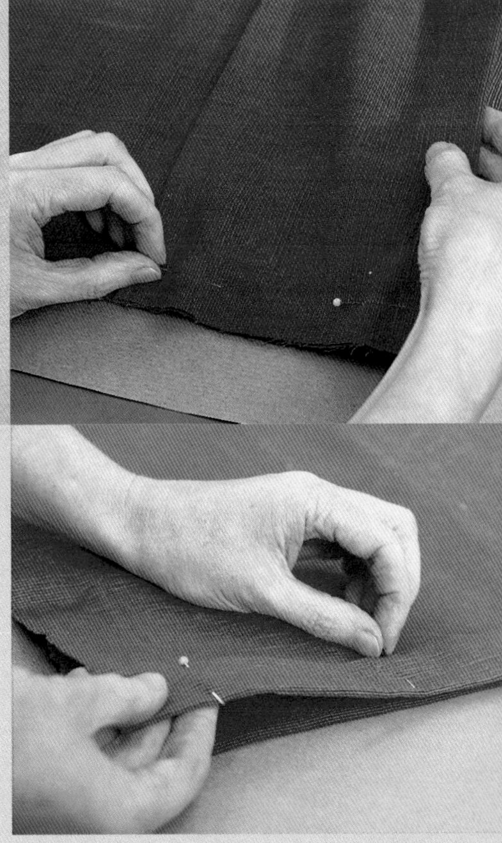

MATERIALS AND EQUIPMENT

- brown paper
- pre-cut foam cushion pad
- washable fabric
- dressmaker's pins
- thin foam sheet
- matching sewing threads
- 2 press studs or 1 zip fastener for each chair seat
- coloured tape
- sewing machine

1 To make the seat covers, cut a brown paper pattern of the pre-cut foam pad, allowing an extra 4cm (1½in) seam allowance all round, depending on the thickness of the pad. Using this as a pattern, cut out two pieces of fabric for each chair.

2 Pin two contrasting colours of fabric right sides together. Machine stitch around the edge, leaving an opening large enough to insert the pad. Hem both sides of the opening and add two press studs or a zip fastener.

3 Turn the cushion covers right out. Stitch a length of coloured tape on either side for tying the cushions to the chair frames.

4 To make the back cushions, it is important to measure each chair individually. Cut a piece of fabric the width of the chair back plus 1cm (½in) seam allowance on both sides, and 1½ times the length of the seat back plus 1cm (½in) seam allowance. Fold back the extra half-length and turn over 2.5cm (1in) to make a hem. This pocket will hold the foam when the cushion is on the chair.

5 Cut a piece of contrasting fabric the width of the chair plus 1cm (½in) seam allowance on both sides, and the length of the seat back plus an extra 2.5cm (1in) to make a hem. Pin the two pieces right sides together, adjusting if necessary until they match exactly. Machine stitch the top and sides. Cut a piece of thin foam sheet to fit the cover and insert it in the pocket. Turn the cover right side out.

VARIATION

As a variation, you can add a second pocket to the back cushion for storing an individual place setting and napkin. Stitch this extra pocket on to the fabric before pinning the sides together.

TILED TRAY TABLE

Many softwood furniture designs intended for use indoors can be customized and weatherproofed for the garden, and a low butler's tray table makes an ideal surface for serving food and drinks. The table is painted with a tough exterior finish, then covered with a loose layer of ceramic tiles to provide a heatproof surface and to give it extra weight for added stability. Odd tiles can be bought very cheaply at DIY stores and tile specialists, but they must all be the same size and thickness. The frame folds flat and the tiles are removable, so the table can be moved indoors in the winter.

MATERIALS AND EQUIPMENT

- sandpaper
- damp cloth
- medium decorator's paintbrush
- water-based undercoat
- coloured exterior-finish paint
- ceramic tiles
- tile-cutter (optional)

1 Lightly sand the surface of the table to give a good key for the undercoat.

2 Wipe down with a damp cloth to remove any dust. Paint the entire tray and frame with undercoat, taking care not to leave any gaps that could allow water to penetrate the finish. Leave to dry completely, then apply a coat of exterior-finish paint.

3 You will probably not find tiles that will exactly fit the tray, so some will need to be cut with a tile-cutter. Alternatively, tiles can be professionally cut, a service available at most specialist tile stores.

Soft chalky blue blends well with all natural garden tones and this colour palette of tiles emphasizes a hot and bright Mediterranean style.

4 Arrange the tiles in a decorative pattern. As they are only loosely laid, they can easily be re-arranged.

5 If the tray, or any softwood furniture, is intended to be used on a lawn, screw a rubber stop to the bottom of each leg to prevent damp from penetrating the paintwork.

HESSIAN CUSHIONS

Certain fabrics are traditionally associated with outside living – canvas or sailcloth are used for sturdy awnings and canopies, and washable plastic or plasticized cotton make practical tablecloths. Roughly-woven hessian is ideal for outdoor cushion covers as it is hard-wearing and inexpensive. The natural pale biscuit colour co-ordinates well with stone and cement seats, and it also dyes well. Colours such as aubergine, terracotta, inky blue or any shade of leaf green look good outdoors. Washing machine dye is colour-fast and will not permanently stain the machine. Each cushion cover will shrink approximately 5cm (2in) all round during the dyeing, so it is important to allow for this when you are cutting out the fabric.

MATERIALS AND EQUIPMENT

- scissors
- fine hessian
- pillows
- dressmaker's pins
- washing machine dye - 1 pack will dye 500g (1lb) of dry fabric
- 500g (1lb) salt for each pack of dye
- washing powder
- fabric conditioner
- embroidery thread, in a contrast colour
- embroidery needle
- matching sewing thread
- sewing machine

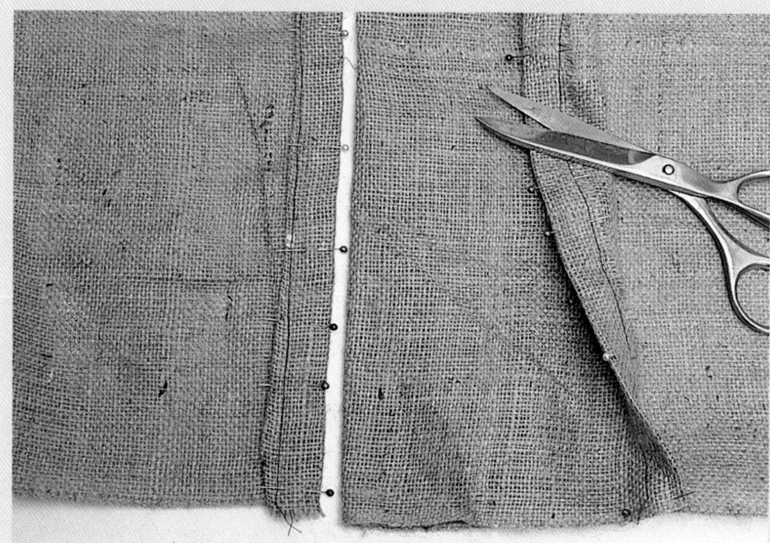

1 Cut a piece of hessian 5cm (2in) larger all round than the pillow. Fold under 2.5cm (1in) along one of the short ends, pin in place and machine stitch. Repeat at the other short end, but this time fold it over again to make a neat hem and topstitch. Fold over this neat hem to a depth of 15cm (6in) and machine both sides of the flap. Fold the hessian in half, with the flap on the outside, and machine stitch down both long sides. Turn the cover inside out. Make as many more covers as you need in the same way.

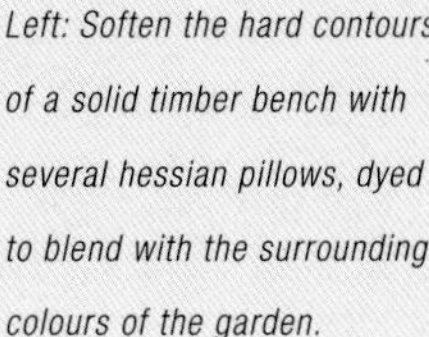

Left: Soften the hard contours of a solid timber bench with several hessian pillows, dyed to blend with the surrounding colours of the garden.

2 Machine wash the hessian covers before dyeing to remove any oils that may affect the process. Machine wash them again with the dye and salt, following the manufacturer's instructions. Finally, machine wash the covers once again using detergent and a generous amount of fabric conditioner to improve the feel of the hessian.

3 Using an embroidery needle and contrast embroidery thread, hand sew a decorative blanket stitch border along all four sides of each cushion cover. Insert the pillows into the covers.

features & focal points

Every outside space should have at least one intriguing feature that makes an impression. A terrace may have a stunning view; one garden may contain a secluded area of peace and privacy; another may include one spectacular tree, or a pergola resplendent with the chandelier-shaped flowers of fragrant wisteria. Features and focal points may be temporary delights or have a degree of seasonal change that continually refreshes their visual impact.

LEFT Natural sculpture like this weather-worn timber and these sea-washed pebbles and shells have a simple Zen-like quality. The simple positioning of every feature shows absolute attention to detail.

Above: A formal gravel garden defined by stone edging makes a contrast in colour and texture to the surrounding soft landscaping and has great impact when viewed from above.

Nearly every element in an outside space can be given some distinctive decorative quality to make it into a stunning feature. A rendered wall painted in a strong colour will arrest the eye and make a sharp contrast with its surroundings. An intricately patterned design of gravel, pebbles, paving and plants is a practical way of combining form and function with decoration. A rose-covered arbour seat offers a profusion of colour and scent in summer, and creates a shady retreat that is sheltered and private. A simple wigwam of bamboo or a distressed metal obelisk may be deemed a garden sculpture, while at the same time providing a self-supporting structure for runner beans or sweet peas. These structures can also look very dramatic in winter, when their naked frames are covered with snow or a sharp frost.

Trees and plants

A single striking object may be all that is required to create dramatic interest, even in the smallest of spaces. A tiny garden could benefit from one beautiful tree or large plant. Tree ferns (*Dicksonia antarctica*), natives of the temperate rainforests of Australasia, are hardy in mild, sheltered areas, prefer shade and need protection from winds. They are ideal for urban gardens, and because they do not have any roots but receive all their moisture and nutrients from their fronds and upper trunk, they grow quite happily in containers. A mature specimen will stand some 10m (33ft) tall and its fronds can be 3m (10ft) long.

Other architectural-looking plants include the Chusan palm (*Trachycarpus fortunei*) and the dwarf palm (*Chamaerops humilis*). The dwarf palm is a

Right: This well-established tree is encircled with a seat of wattle fencing made from woven willow and a place to sit and enjoy the view of the landscape beyond the garden.

European native and reaches a height of about 3m (10ft), half the size of the Chusan palm. Tree ferns and palms grow slowly so purchasing a mature specimen is a major investment, but they are living sculptures and will be an elegant, space-saving feature on a small terrace or in a garden room.

Containers are ideal for bamboos as this kind of planting will restrain the invasive habits of many of this species. With rustling leaves that are often strikingly variegated and coloured stems varying from golden yellow to inky black, bamboos thrive in shelter and shade. Grown individually in simple pots or metal containers, they bring a feeling of peacefulness to modern spaces and their reed-like stems have a natural affinity with water. Grown en masse, bamboos create a dramatic jungle through which paths can be cut and clearings made – a private paradise hidden from the outside world. Unlike palms, there are varieties of bamboo that will withstand temperatures well below 20ºC (68ºF), making them a fine evergreen feature in winter.

It is in winter that outside spaces can truly be assessed for the quality of their 'bone structure', and for a tree to earn the status of an ornamental feature it needs to have all-year-round interest. Trees should be assessed for their shape, bark, flowers and fruit, which, unlike non-organic ornaments, will change in colour and form over the seasons. Specialist nurseries will give advice and supply suitable trees, priced according to maturity and size. Numerous varieties of Japanese maple (*Acer palmatum*), ornamental cherry (*Prunus*) and pear (*Pyrus salicifolia* 'Pendula' and *P. calleryana* 'Chanticleer') make an attractive central focus in a gravelled courtyard or a planting pocket in paving. It is often recommended to plant these trees in late October but they have been successfully planted as early as August, when the soil is warmer.

Left: Overhead beams, supported by the building structure and bricked plinths, are softened with wisteria which blossoms in spring and produces a thick shade-giving foliage throughout the summer period.

Below: A metal arbour provides the framework for roses to clamber over and conceals a secluded dining area surrounded by summer-flowering evening scented flowers and aromatic foliage.

Vertical structures

Pergolas, archways and tunnels are usually associated with country gardens, but these shapes are also invaluable in making the best use of limited space in an urban setting. Creating a false ceiling and dividing an area can actually make it appear larger than it really is.

Just as a change of level adds horizontal interest to even the tiniest garden or patio, so too an arch of woven willow can be used to designate one 'room' from another. In winter, the bare brown branches have a sculptural quality, and with careful planting they can be covered with an early flowering clematis followed by another variety that blooms in summer or autumn. Freshly planted willow stems also take root quickly and will burst into leaf in the spring.

Treated rustic poles or roughly sawn timbers blend well into natural or wildlife gardens, while rendered pillars and simply styled metalwork are better suited to modern or formal spaces. Metal arches and pergolas can be used with great effect to link a building with a garden or patio. Wooden or metal beams can be supported between a house and a free-standing pole or timber upright by means of joist hangers, to create a verandah. This offers semi-shade and privacy from upstairs windows and adjoining properties. This style of structure is very common in southern France and Italy, where the fronts of many houses are shaded from the sun and sheltered from wind and rain.

Whether attached to a building or free-standing, a verandah must be constructed with appropriate materials and firm foundations, particularly if it is to be covered with perennial climbers. Many climbing plants grow at an amazing rate and their sheer weight can make flimsy structures collapse unless the supports are sunk into concrete or proprietary metal spikes, which will protect them from contact with the wet soil. It is also important to make sure that the overhead structure is high enough to accommodate foliage such as the low-hanging flowers of wisteria or laburnum.

Features from the past

Many older houses are furnished and decorated with a reference to the past, often to the period when they were first built. Architectural details such as fireplaces are often retained and incorporated into the design scheme, even though their relevance has been superseded by central heating. In these homes it may be desirable to continue this style with formal, traditional outside spaces featuring eighteenth-century Italian-style balconies and balustrades, and ornate metalwork furniture, arches and screens in the spirit of the great French châteaux. Geometry, proportion and perfect symmetry are features that are typical of this style, so the look can be created quite simply by placing classically styled urns, either in pairs or singly, at the centre of a paved area, surrounded by an immaculate clipped box hedge.

Sundials are a traditional form of exterior decoration dating back some 5,000 years. They only tell local time so, unless you have one made for you, an old sundial will probably be purely decorative. Other garden antiques such as terracotta rhubarb forcers, French glass cloches or maraîchères (used to protect tender seedlings), or Victorian watering cans, appeal to those with an interest in the past. They all offer authentic traditional garden decoration and may serve to prompt the beginning of an addiction to collecting.

Huge pots and urns are very versatile garden ornaments. Standing alone, they give sculptural relief in the midst of lush planting or in isolation at the end of a path. They may be capacious enough to hold a small tree, or to be filled with stones or sand an as effective foundation for anchoring a pole to support an awning or canopy. The most humble of terracotta pots becomes a work of personal expression when painted or covered with a mosaic of broken china or sea shells pressed into cement. Beachcombing for shells and small stones with holes will also provide natural ingredients for a hanging mobile or windchime strung together with garden twine or transparent fishing line.

Left: Voluminous water and olive oil jars are grouped together here to give visual impact. They are naturally decorated with the cast shadow patterns by a nearby conifer.

Disguising the utilities

Some garden objects are dull or even plain ugly, and they need a decorative treatment that is more of a disguise than a focus. Sheds, gas and oil tanks, dustbins, compost heaps, even drainpipes do not have to be eyesores.

Garden sheds are essential as they provide the only storage space for tools, furniture, pots and equipment, but they can be organized so every inch of space is used. Tools can be hung on wall racks, furniture stashed in simple frames attached to the ceiling, and rows of shelves can be provided for pots and equipment. Fertilizers and chemicals have to be stored carefully, so ensure that the lids are tightly closed and that they are placed well out of the reach of children and animals.

If you are buying a new shed it may be practical to choose something more capacious and decorative, which could be used as a summerhouse as well as for storage. A well-constructed, insulated garden room is particularly appealing to people who run a business from home, but need the psychological transition of leaving home to start work each day. Assuming that such a profession requires little more than chair and desk space, a summerhouse or shed with at least one window can be customized into a small but perfectly adequate workroom. Power for lighting, heat and equipment can be connected to the main building, and should ideally be installed by a qualified electrician to ensure that all the safety precautions are observed. Outside, wood paints or stains will quickly transform

Above: This raised terrace creates a warm suntrap between house and garden. The terrace is subtly blended by painting the walls, deck joists and furniture all the same colour.

Right: Pennisetum villosum *with its ethereal drooping flowerheads that move in the slightest breeze and contrast effectively with the static sculptures of rounded stones held erect on silvery metal spikes.*

Below: A simple but effective idea. Recycled blue bottles pushed onto the spiked tops of a weather-worn fence glitter in the sun, forming a colourful and decorative border and attractively soften the fence's contours.

the exterior, and the building will blend into its surroundings if you attach trellis or wire supports to the sides and grow evergreen climbers or wall shrubs. A thick blanket of foliage will hide the shed and will also provide extra insulation.

Similar techniques can be applied to other vital but unattractive utilities such as dustbins and tanks. Enclose them with trellis or fencing, covered with climbers as further decorative camouflage. Alternatively, plant an evergreen hedge of common holly (*Ilex aquifolium*), bamboo or yew (*Taxus baccata*). In fact, almost any woody shrub, evergreen or deciduous, that produces strong secondary growth from its cut stems is suitable for hedging.

Garden furniture can sometimes be adapted to create hidden storage for unsightly objects – a huge pot can serve as a container for smaller pots or a hosepipe, an old beehive can be converted into a

compost bin or garden store cupboard, and a garden seat could be constructed around a box with a hinged lid. The exterior of a building can often be blighted with pipework but fast-growing climbers such as ivies, many vines, wisteria and clematis will cover the offending items in a few years. Some climbers appreciate wire supports but many are self-clinging and, unless the property is extremely old with crumbling mortar, they will do no harm to the masonry.

Outdoor art

Any purely decorative object you decide to include in your outdoor space will be determined by your personal taste and style. Many artists and sculptors now specialize in garden ornaments and art and craft galleries increasingly exhibit their work.

Instead of a simple bench, a garden seat could be a unique piece created by a designer-maker to be functional as well as aesthetically pleasing. Artists such as Andy Goldsworthy have inspired others to work with natural materials and his influence on modern garden culture encourages us to look at leaves, twigs and stones in a very different light. Garden ornaments such as birds and animals fashioned from wire or reclaimed materials can be witty and amusing but still have integrity. Traditional topiary figures were laboriously fashioned by clipping box or yew, but ready-made frames in the shapes of animals or simple cones, spheres and spirals have given us a short cut to creating designs out of ivy or clematis. One step further is to introduce living ornaments such as exotic breeds of chicken or fish. In large country gardens, geese were traditionally kept to scare off intruders, but a smaller garden may be able to accommodate a pair of tame ducks that will organically keep the slug population in check.

Left: This contemporary sculpture exactly captures the effect of tall reeds and arching grasses. It would make an ideal permanent focal point of a small pond or a modern water feature.

PAINTED BIRD BOX

MATERIALS AND EQUIPMENT

- tape measure
- soft pencil
- approximately 1m (1yd) length of old floorboard
- set square
- saw
- drill, with hole-cutter attachment
- 10cm (4in) length of dowelling
- hammer
- 35mm (1½in) galvanized clout nails
- several small pieces of driftwood
- 30mm (1¼in) copper clout nails
- medium-sized decorator's paintbrush
- emulsion paint, in 2 contrast colours
- medium-grade sandpaper
- wood wax
- metal-cutters or tin snips
- piece of zinc roofing
- a length of 2mm (.08in) galvanized wire, for hanging the box

Encourage birds to visit your garden with this delightful bird box, which requires only basic carpentry skills. Alternatively, you can buy an unfinished bird box and paint it in your own colour scheme, then add details such as a chimney, weathervane and flags.

Most of the materials used here are reclaimed from skips and beachcombing expeditions and for the paint you can use old cans or buy small tester pots. No two bird boxes will be the same, and two or three hung on a tree (or an outside wall out of the reach of cats) will make colourful focal points in a garden.

1 Using a pencil, mark two identical 'house shapes' (an equilateral triangle on top of a square) on the floorboard. Use a set square to check the 45° angles on the triangle. Cut out with a saw then cut another piece for the base. Using a drill with a hole-cutter attachment, cut a large hole in the centre front for the entrance and a small hole the diameter of the dowelling immediately below it. The size of the entrance hole depends on the birds you wish to attract.

Left: Extra perches can be glued or nailed on to the bird box. Here a tiny piece of sheet copper has been cut to make a fluttering pendant.

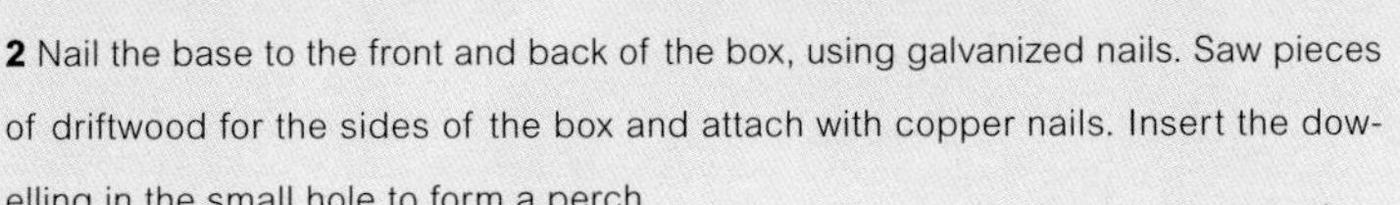

2 Nail the base to the front and back of the box, using galvanized nails. Saw pieces of driftwood for the sides of the box and attach with copper nails. Insert the dowelling in the small hole to form a perch.

3 Paint the outside of the box with emulsion paint and leave to dry, then paint a contrast-coloured coat of emulsion on top. When completely dry, rub down the surface with sandpaper until the paint colour underneath begins to show through and the heads of the copper nails are visible. Paint around the entrance again with the first colour so that the birds will see it. Apply a generous coat of wax over all the exterior surfaces.

VARIATION

Adapt the basic shape to make different sizes and styles, based on vernacular architecture and fantasy houses from imagination or memory.

4 Using metal-cutters or tin snips, cut the zinc roofing to give a good overlap on all sides of the box. Place the zinc over the box and crease it along the centre to match the top. Mark the middle of the crease and also two places where the zinc roof will meet the sides of the box. Remove the zinc and punch holes with a nail through the marks. Knot one end of the wire and thread it up through the centre hole, for hanging the bird box. Finally, replace the zinc roof on the box, lining up the holes at the sides, and attach it with copper nails.

RUSTIC MIRROR

Mirrors multiply light, giving it an energy that will bring a dark corner of the garden to life. Even a small mirror can be positioned to accentuate another feature or the texture of the bark on a tree, but do not make the mirror too large or place it where birds may be disorientated and fly into it.

Reclaimed timber such as old floor joists has a robust, chunky character that is ideal for outdoors. Do not worry about small gaps where the timbers join as they contribute to the effect and will be disguised by paint. If the wood you are using has not already been treated, apply a coat of preservative before assembling the frame.

You can decorate the finished mirror with shells, small stones, tiny mosaic tiles or glass beads threaded onto galvanized or copper wire.

Right: Hung in the centre of a wooden trellis panel, the mirror blends with its surroundings and reflects a tiny section of the garden beyond.

MATERIALS AND EQUIPMENT

- 2 x 25cm (10in) lengths and 2 x 60cm (2ft) lengths of reclaimed timber, approximately 5cm (2in) thick and 10cm (4in) wide
- set square
- waterproof wood glue
- hammer
- 75mm (3in) round wire nails
- medium-sized decorator's paintbrush
- white acrylic primer
- fine-grade sandpaper
- wood wax
- safety goggles
- drill, with rebate attachment
- 18 x 51cm (7 x 20in) piece of mirror glass
- glazing sprigs (small, specialized nails to hold the mirror in place)
- 30mm (1¼in) galvanized screws
- a length of 2mm (.08in) galvanized wire, for hanging the mirror

1 Place one long and one short piece of timber together at right angles, checking the angle with a set square. Smear a little glue along the inside edges where the two meet then lay one piece on a level surface with the other piece vertically on top, edge to edge. Hammer in two nails on either side at an angle, so that they secure the wood underneath. Repeat with the other two timbers to make a box frame.

2 Paint the frame with acrylic primer and leave to dry. Rub with sandpaper until the grain of the wood begins to show through. Apply a generous layer of wax to give an effective waterproof coating.

VARIATION

Here two shades of green emulsion paint have been sponged onto the frame, exactly matching the colours of the variegated ivy surrounding it. The candle is held in place using the coiled wire holder on pages 84–86.

3 Wearing safety goggles and using a drill with a rebate attachment make a rebate on the back of the frame in which the mirror glass will sit comfortably. Alternatively, take the frame to a DIY centre and ask them to cut a rebate.

4 Carefully slide the mirror glass into place and secure firmly with glazing sprigs and plenty of glue around all the edges. Insert a screw on either side of the top back of the frame and link a piece of wire between the two for hanging the mirror.

lighting

There are numerous ways to make an outside space take on a magical appearance at night. Choose from the simple glow of a nightlight to the romantic twinkle of trees swathed in fairy lights or as an alternative, the sophisticated electrical schemes that are integrated into walls and flooring. The judicious use of artificial light can silhouette trees and plants, dramatize a water feature and create an intimate dining space.

LEFT The most evocative and romantic form of outdoor lighting is also the most ancient. Candlelight is warm, flattering to faces and has a hypnotic quality that induces calm and relaxation.

Above: Nothing artificial can compare to the beauty of natural light and the way it brings static objects to life, giving them a gentle and beguiling luminosity.

The light an outdoor space receives depends on the aspect – the direction in which the site faces. The amount of sunlight will vary depending on the time of year and the amount of shade will be affected by overhanging trees, high walls and nearby buildings. Understanding the effects of light and shade should be an important part of your design for both people and plants.

A simple compass reading will determine where the sun rises and sets, and careful observation on a clear day will indicate the sunniest areas and which parts are subject to shade. Armed with this information, you can then designate the best places for seating and dining, as well as choosing which are the most appropriate plants to grow. Remember that the direction of the prevailing winds is also a factor, so even if there is plenty of sunlight you may still need to provide shelter for people and delicate plants.

After the sun has set, artificial lighting provides a dramatic way to extend the potential of the outside space, whether it be a small terrace or a large garden that is full of trees and shrubs. The problem with artificial outdoor lighting is that the overall effect all too often looks false and even garish. It is therefore important to plan the lighting as carefully as the rest of the space, and to incorporate different kinds of light in your design. The two most common reasons for using outside illumination are security and aesthetics, and you may need to combine these seemingly disparate criteria in one lighting scheme.

Above: The shadows cast by bamboo leaves make a decorative pattern against a sunlit fence. This is constructed from bamboo canes and held in place by poles.

In the winter the outside space is viewed mainly from the inside looking out and can be lit accordingly. At the height of summer many people enjoy gardening in the evening, which may be the only time when the temperature is cool enough for tasks such as weeding. There is also something very relaxing and soothing about watering a garden by the light of the moon, either real or artfully created.

Following the sun

In perfect conditions, it makes sense to link the outside space and the interior of the house by means of a terrace, creating a seamless transition between the two. However, in many situations, and particularly in an urban location, the sunniest and least shaded area may in fact be the one farthest away from the property.

As well as being the obvious location for relaxing and entertaining, a sunny patch at the end of the garden can also become the site for a more permanent structure. Set apart from the house, an outside room has the attraction of a complete retreat, providing it is adequately equipped with power sources and linked to the home with some form of hard surface.

Before laying a path, consider the types of power you need such as conduits for lighting cables and for an exterior electrical socket. If you plan ahead in this way, an outdoor room can be as user-friendly as any indoor room, with the means to plug into music, make coffee and toast a sandwich.

Right: The basic framework of a garden is most apparent In the winter months. The frosted white lawn shown here emphasizes the shadow patterns of the bare branched trees and the herringbone design of the trellis.

Candlelight

When the weather is warm, outdoor living and entertaining can be extended long after sunset. Pressing a switch for instant electric light is convenient but the most attractive source of artificial light, both inside and out, is undoubtedly candles. Their gently flickering glow is romantic and flattering to both faces and food, and it is the cheapest and easiest form of lighting to use.

For a very small financial outlay, you can put scores of nightlights in jam jars or small glass tumblers. Suspend them on wires from branches or the horizontal bars of trellis, line them up in rows along the top of a wall, tuck them into the corners of step risers or make a continuous snake along the contours of a path. Metal storm lanterns are also excellent outdoors because, as with glass jars, the flame is protected. Many designs are available, from the highly decorative shapes made in India and Mexico to the more utilitarian styles found at camping suppliers.

A patio or terrace with a solid or beamed roof will provide a support for a candle-lit chandelier, but it needs to be completely protected from any wind if the candles are to stay alight. If the evening is completely still, push a generous group of candles or garden flares into a terracotta pot or galvanized bucket filled with sand. Garden flares are designed to withstand a reasonable amount of wind and will burn for several hours. Always be careful with outdoor candles and flares in case a gust of wind causes a spurt of hot wax, or burns plants or furniture. Naked flames must never be left unattended and should be extinguished with a candle-snuffer.

Many garden flares are impregnated with citronella oil, which discourages the mosquitoes and gnats that are attracted by candles on summer evenings. The distinctive smell does not appeal to everyone, so instead you can vaporize lemongrass essential oil in an oil burner. Another alternative is eucalyptus oil – it is planted in swampy areas in North Africa to deter mosquitoes from breeding.

The marriage of candlelight and water is a simple, inexpensive and very effective way to create some atmospheric lighting. The still surface of a small pond, for example, will come alive at night if you decorate it with an enchanting flotilla of floating candles. Or on a smaller scale, you can create a beautiful table centrepiece with a shallow bowl of water containing floating scented candles. For a touch of romance, add some fragrant rose heads pinned on to tiny corks to keep them afloat. An additional benefit of combining candles with water is that the flames will be safely extinguished when the candles burn down.

Above (top): These concertina-style Japanese paper lanterns offer practical protection from the wind.

Above (bottom): This more contemporary alternative uses fireproofed paper bags that are half filled with sand to make a firm base for a nightlight.

Left: During the day cool air flows freely through the triangular recesses of a wall section resembling a fretwork window screen. These tiny shelves then provide individual niches for glass lanterns to illuminate the terrace by night. The perfume wafting from a bowl of floating candles is enhanced with the fresh scent of rose petals.

Security lighting

This kind of lighting is primarily for deterring intruders. It is usually activated by movement and is linked to an alarm, which is clearly audible from inside the property. To be effective, it needs to highlight vulnerable areas such as the perimeter of the area and the exits and entrances.

It is advisable to have a separate system for security lighting, which can be activated when the property is unoccupied and is operated by a master switch in a convenient place inside the house.

Creating a mood

Atmospheric lighting needs to be more subtle. You can make an outside space look as though it is lit naturally by the moon and stars, or you can sensitively accent light it with uplighters and spotlights. If a garden has a large, mature tree, this offers the potential to create a night-time canopy of tiny lights resembling twinkling stars. Alternatively, larger downlighters can be used to make shadow patterns on the ground. The electric cables that feed these lights are best wound around and attached to the tree trunk with plastic plant ties, fixed with stainless steel nails. The plant ties will allow the cables room for movement as the trunk grows and expands. Where the cable meets the ground, it should be buried in a protective conduit and run back to its source along a route where it is unlikely to be disturbed by cultivation. Remember that the positioning of the light fittings must be accessible so that you can replace bulbs, but long-life outdoor bulbs (lasting about 24,000 hours) will make maintenance much easier.

The most unobtrusive method of lighting the ground where you are likely to walk is with recessed uplighters. Such light fittings emit a glow that is bright enough to clearly see the surrounding ground without creating a blinding upward shaft of light. An economical method of concealing uplighters is to place them in small terracotta pots so that the cable runs through the drainage holes.

Some garden lightsare fitted to a rigid plastic spike so that they can be angled to highlight shrubs or ornaments. It is a great advantage to be able to highlight different parts of your outdoor space at different times of year. One effective mobile system is provided by solar-powered garden lights; the sunlight charges a battery via a solar panel, which in turn lights the lamp after dark.

Above: This is a contemporary lighting scheme with uplighters and recessed downlighters that are virtually invisible. The subtle effect integrates the glass-fronted house with the exterior.

Left: Functional lighting can also be used to give a decorative quality to an outside area. This row of glare-free lights illuminates the flight of brick steps.

Below: A vertical structure such as this can be constructed and used to provide a conduit through which a power circuit can be concealed.

The technicalities

Artificial lighting is a science – but not one to be intimidated by. Installation is best left to a professional electrician, but the effects also need to be designed to suit the style of the garden or terrace.

Low-voltage circuits are ideal for small outside spaces where only short cable runs are required. The system is fitted with a transformer which lowers the voltage, making the supply safer. Low-voltage lights tend to be smaller and, if strategically placed, are barely visible during the day.

However well you have planned your lighting, it is wise to keep a record of all the power circuits in the space. This will be particularly useful for future owners. The best route for power circuits is to follow the perimeter of a terrace or alongside paths, which is the logical place to install lighting.

Because of their location, outdoor lights must be completely weatherproof. Many bathroom fittings and the heavy-duty lights found at ship's chandlers are also practical in an outdoor space.

RECYCLED GLASS LANTERNS

Candlelight is especially evocative in a garden space, where the flickering flames create a magical atmosphere and give instant light. Hang a row of these lovely lanterns from metal butcher's hooks across a terrace or from the branches of a tree. However, take care to space them out in case a gust of wind causes them to clash together and shatter.

Apart from a bottle-cutter, the only materials needed are empty glass bottles and wire. White wine and mineral water bottles work best as the candlelight is visible through the clear glass. The lanterns become very hot when the candles are alight so wait until they have burnt out before attempting to remove the glass, or use oven gloves. Never leave burning candles unattended, even in the garden.

VARIATION

Without the wire and with the addition of a metal brioche tin, the bottle makes a storm lantern for a tiny candle. Make sure the surface you stand it on is heat-resistant.

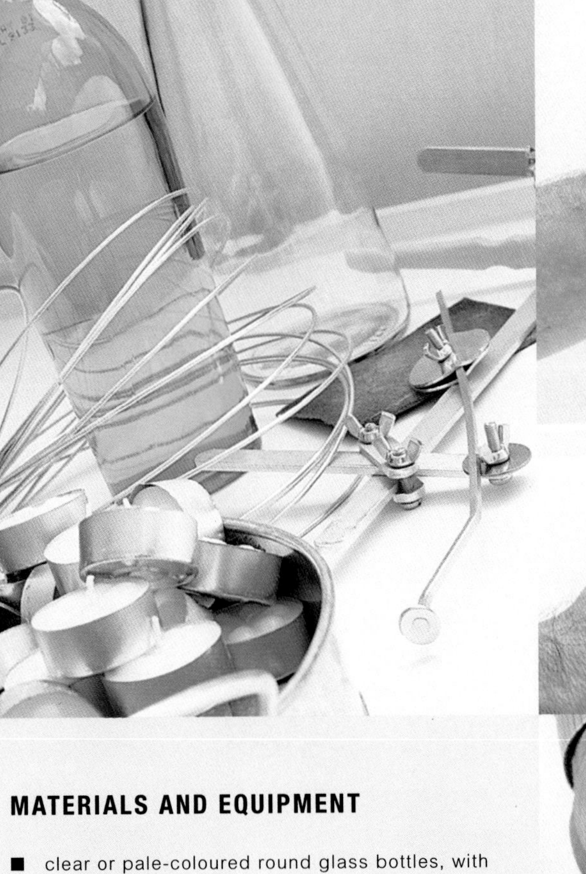

MATERIALS AND EQUIPMENT

- clear or pale-coloured round glass bottles, with clearly defined necks
- bottle-cutter
- coarse emery paper or a small silicon-carbide stone (as used to sharpen knives)
- wire-cutters
- a length 2mm (.08in) galvanized wire
- small tin can, approximately 5cm (2in) diameter
- nightlights
- pliers

1 Wash and dry the bottles, removing any labels. Adjust the height of the bottle-cutter to where you wish to cut the bottle. Tighten all the screws then revolve the blade and make one continuous score line. Experiment on spare bottles if necessary until you perfect the technique.

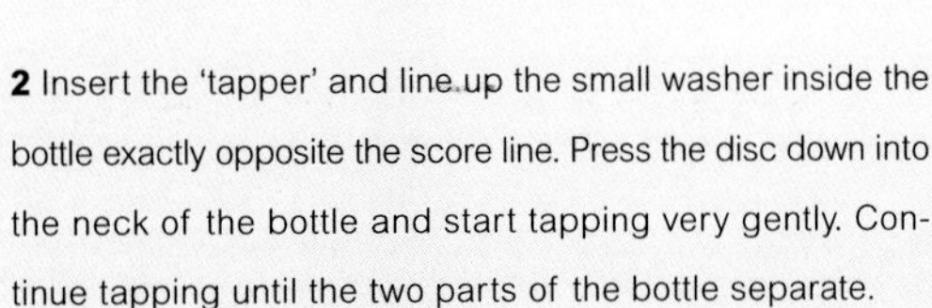

2 Insert the 'tapper' and line up the small washer inside the bottle exactly opposite the score line. Press the disc down into the neck of the bottle and start tapping very gently. Continue tapping until the two parts of the bottle separate.

3 The cut end of the bottle is razor sharp so rub it down carefully with emery paper. Alternatively, use a small silicon-carbide stone to smooth the rim.

4 Cut a piece of wire approximately twice the length of the bottle and straighten it as much as possible. Push it up inside the bottle then make a double kink to hold the wire in place inside the neck.

5 Twist the lower end of the wire around a small can to make symmetric coils, rather like a metal bedspring. This will be the candle-holder for the nightlight.

6 Adjust the lower coils by winding them more tightly until the nightlight fits snugly and is perfectly level. Insert the wire and nightlight into the bottle. Using pliers, twist the top of the wire to make a hook for hanging.

Left: Even in a breeze, the lantern stays alight and the flickering flames cast attractive reflections through the glass.

SCENTED CHANDELIER

Fill a hanging basket with tiny fairy lights and sweet-scented plants to softly illuminate and perfume a terrace. Glass droplets tied with invisible fishing line sparkle in the lights and chime softly, like the sound of chinking glasses.

Ideally, plant up the basket when the plants are in full bud so that the flowers will open in situ. Once they have faded, the jasmine can be planted outside if protected from the frost but the stephanotis, which originates from Madagascar, will need a minimum temperature of 15ºC (59ºF).

MATERIALS AND EQUIPMENT

- lights, with transformer
- metal hanging basket
- bucket
- thin fuse wire or florist's wire
- moss
- scissors
- basket liner or garden gauze
- 2 *Stephanotis floribunda* plants
- 3 *Jasminum polyanthum* plants
- transparent fishing line
- glass droplets

1 Low-voltage outdoor lights must only be plugged into a socket that is indoors and protected by an approved circuit-breaker. Unravel the lights and ensure that they are working. Turn the lights off at the mains when replacing faulty bulbs. Place the hanging basket in a bucket to keep it steady, then wire the lights to the sides and base of the basket. Take care to keep the bulbs separate from each other.

2 Line the basket with a layer of moss and push firmly into the sides. Cut a circle of liner or gauze that will slightly overlap the top of the basket.

3 The single stem of a stephanotis plant is usually trained over a wire frame. Remove this carefully and re-plant in the basket. Wind the stem around the perimeter of the basket, holding it securely with wire but without tying it so tight that it damages the stem. Add the other stephanotis and the jasmine plants.

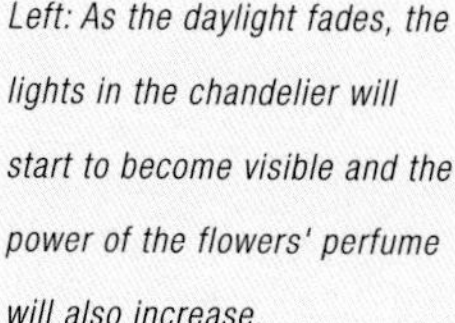

Left: As the daylight fades, the lights in the chandelier will start to become visible and the power of the flowers' perfume will also increase.

4 Switch on the fairy lights and ensure that they are not touching. Then switch the lights off and hang the basket in position. Switch them on again and thread a length of fishing line on to each glass droplet and suspend them at differing levels from the sides and bottom of the basket.

water

We have a deep affinity with water. It both stimulates and relaxes our senses and can be a vital element in the contemporary outside room. There is something intrinsically soothing about the sight of reflections on an expanse of still water; the sound of a softly gurgling fountain, bubbling up amongst smooth stones; or the sensation of sitting in a hot tub under the stars. Water can create excitement with sound and stimulation or it can be used to induce a cool atmosphere of calming relaxation.

LEFT As this sheet of water cascades from a simple spout, it recreates the sound of a waterfall and radiates sprays of tiny droplets caught sparkling in the sunlight.

Water is a great and universal source of attraction. The ancient gardens of the Islamic world symbolized paradise on earth, as instructed in the writings of the Koran, and featured the same rhythmic geometrical patterns found on oriental carpets. Those gardens represented an escape from the harshness of the desert, so water was an essential element, cooling the air and creating much-needed humidity. Fine examples of traditional Islamic water and shade gardens can still be seen at the Alhambra in Granada, Spain, and at the Palace of Almudaina in Palma, Majorca. Although created more than 500 years ago, their engineering and their classic lines and perfect proportions continue to influence landscape design today.

The pleasure we derive from having a bath or shower, and experiencing the sight and smell of the sea, confirms the close affinity we feel with water. It stimulates and relaxes all our senses, restoring our sense of well-being. Contemporary bathroom design has moved on from its functional roots to embrace a more eastern influence, where time is taken to enjoy the simple pleasures of bathing.

This fascination with water extends outdoors, where designers, architects and sculptors are using modern technology and materials to create fantastic effects. A contemporary water feature has now risen to the top of the list of popular focal points and ornaments for the garden.

Right: Designed with careful precision and related to the proportions of the architecture, a swimming pool is both a luxurious outdoor bathroom and a still blue surface reflecting the ever-changing sky.

Left: A sybaritical delight. The perfect inside and outside bathroom where you can bathe in the internal shade or shower in the fresh air and sunshine.

Below: A non-slip border between the edge of the swimming pool and the raised deck platform provides a well-considered safety element.

Outdoor pools and tubs

Depending on the space available, the benefits of water can be enjoyed outside in a heated swimming pool, a hot tub fitted with powerful jets for muscle-soothing hydrotherapy or a simple outdoor shower for refreshing drenches.

The construction of a swimming pool is best left to professionals and careful consideration needs to be given to its design, its relationship to surrounding buildings and safety provisions. In hot climates where a pool is the centre of an outside lifestyle virtually all year round, it makes sense to site it near to the house. Even in cooler climes, if the pool is sufficiently heated it can be used when there is snow on the ground, providing there is only a short dash to a warm interior. Whatever the size of the pool, it must be regarded as a high-maintenance feature with continuous running costs for the filtration and skimmer systems, plus additional expenses if the water is to be kept permanently heated.

Smaller projects such as a hot tub require little space. A tub could be integrated into the design for a small, secluded courtyard or positioned on a roof terrace that is not overlooked – privacy is an important requirement for outdoor bathing. Inspiration for the design of a hot tub can be found in traditional Japanese bathrooms, which often feature natural materials such as stone and wood that are appropriate in an exterior setting.

Above: A natural pond and wildlife paradise is all but concealed by the dense cover of moisture-loving plants, particularly alchemilla mollis, *which cascades over the stone edges, providing a place for birds and animals to drink.*

Ponds

A gravelled garden is ideal for installing the simplest of all water features, a shallow pond, with the minimum of disruption. Traditional Japanese gardens often combine a water feature with gravel or slate 'Paddlestones', which were originally naturally smoothed in rivers but are now produced industrially in tumbling machines. The advantage of a loose-stoned or grassed garden is that any electric cables required for lighting or a pump can be conveniently concealed underneath. Ideally, conduits to carry power cables should be included in the initial plans for an outside space. It would be inconceivable to build a house without making provision for plumbing and electricity, yet these vital elements are often overlooked when planning a garden. If you are laying a paved area, it costs very little to include a length of plastic conduit beneath the paving through which power cables can be fed at a later stage.

Designing an outside space to include a water feature will have a dramatic effect on the style of planting. It will open up the possibilities of using moisture-loving and marginal plants, as well as those that require total submersion of their roots and those that float on the surface of the water.

High-quality long-life PVC (polyvinyl chloride) fabrics and butyl (isobutylene isoprene rubber) liners have made the construction of informal pools a simple DIY project that can be completed in a few hours. Bought by the metre, these liners are guaranteed to last for at least 20 years and, being mostly black, they give excellent surface reflections. Using a liner, you can design a formal pond with straight edges and vertical sides topped with stone slabs or sympathetic paving. These need to overhang the water enough to conceal the liner beneath. Alternatively, you can create a more free-form shape with stepped shelves around the perimeter for marginal and bog plants, or a sloping 'pebble beach' edge where birds and animals can drink and bathe.

If toddlers and young children play in the garden, great care must be taken to ensure that any water feature is perfectly safe. A small pond can be filled with large stones to just below the waterline until the children are older. A deep pond can be

Left: Water is a major feature in the Japanese garden. The ponds are often relatively shallow and are described by the term kage ike *or mirror pond. This is due to the underside curvature of a bridge being reflected in the still water below.*

covered with a removable fine metal mesh which, if positioned just below the water surface, is not too obtrusive. Such safety guards may also be necessary if you keep fish and there is a danger they may poached by herons.

Installing a fountain in a small reservoir is an attractive way to avoid the potential dangers of open water. A submersible pump sits at the bottom of a lined hole or pond and draws water in through an integral filter, pumping it out in a range of different spray patterns that can be adjusted to imitate the subtle gurgle of a natural spring. Standing the pump on a brick ensures that it is kept on a flat surface and prevents any dirt or sludge from the bottom of the pond interfering with the pump mechanism. Most pumps are designed to run off mains electricity and their cables, which are best laid underground, need to be protected inside a sturdy conduit, usually a rigid plastic pipe. The installation is best carried out by a qualified electrician, who will also be able to install a circuit-breaker if you do not already have one.

The only drawback of a sunken pond is if the site has a naturally high water-table. After heavy winter rainfall the level of underground water may raise the liner, causing it to balloon up out of the pond. In such circumstances, it may be wiser to construct a raised pond or series of wide channels connected by concrete or timber-decking walkways. Wooden decking has a natural affinity with water and creates a nautical style reminiscent of narrow piers and jetties in sheltered coastal harbours. If you construct the decking so that it overhangs the water, this will make the pond appear larger and will give a crisp contemporary shape.

A raised pond can also incorporate a wide edge of stone or timber broad enough for seating. If the site is sloping or uneven, a series of wooden decks would make an attractive link between a series of sunken and raised pools, in which the water is pumped and recycled from the lowest pond to the top. Ambitious projects like these are best carried out using professional help and advice.

Above: Nature can provide a wonderful source of inspiration for the design of contemporary water features. The bank of rounded pebbles contrasts with the radiating frame of slate.

A precious resource

Water is too valuable a resource to waste, so every gardener needs to consider how best to utilize and conserve it. Most garden plants can in fact survive short spells of drought because their roots stretch deep down into the ground and, with a suitable mulch, very little of the water in the soil is lost through evaporation. But containers, especially those with a porous surface such as terracotta, require watering as much as twice a day in summer. It would be foolhardy to plan a garden without an outside water source, especially if it is on a roof where the drying effects of the wind can be as harmful as hot sun.

Watering a small container garden by hand can be soothing, but it is also sensible to have a back-up so that you are not obliged to stay at home all summer. Modern irrigation systems are designed to water specific areas and types of planting, and can be linked to a feed option providing exact amounts of fertilizer. Many of the more sophisticated systems have environmental sensory devices that can detect when there has been sufficient rainfall or if there is a risk of freezing. Even a basic irrigation system, in which water is delivered to individual pots by a web of surface pipes attached to tiny sprays, can be connected to a 24-hour timer.

Left: In a tiny enclosed courtyard, the flowing water keeps good 'chi'-energy -moving and reflects against the metallic plinth. The brimming pool creates a pleasant and cooling atmosphere.

Above: Underwater lighting can illuminate the bottom of a pool and reveal a mysterious world hidden below the surface, creating a wonderful environment for nocturnal swimming.

CONTAINER POND

This is an ideal water feature for a raised deck or roof terrace where a permanent water feature would be impractical. Choose a container that suits the style and size of your space – a cool grey steel container looks very modern, but you could equally well use a shallow stone bowl or glazed ceramic jar. The silvery colour of the container used here makes a bold contrast to a planting scheme of various shades and textures of foliage.

The plants are individually planted so it is easy to rearrange or replace them. This scheme is designed for a warm environment, but in colder climates tender specimens can be wintered indoors or treated as annuals and bought fresh each year.

MATERIALS AND EQUIPMENT

- selection of marginal and aquatic plants
- plastic pots to suit the size of the plants
- sterile clay-based loam or aquatic compost, well sieved
- aquatic gravel
- polythene bags
- stainless steel container
- rubber gloves
- clean bricks
- underwater light (optional)

PLANTS

- Burr-reed or prairie cord grass (*Spartina pectinata* 'Aureo-marginata'), a hardy marginal plant that should be positioned with the top of the pot just below water level.
- Water lettuce (*Pistia stratiotes*), a tender aquatic plant which will float at surface level in water 10–45cm (4–18in) deep.
- Scouring rush or mare's horsetail (*Equisetum hyemale*) should be planted in 15cm (6in) of water.
- Umbrella plant (*Cyperus alternifolius*), a tender marginal plant that should be planted at water level. It may be treated as a house plant in winter in a warm, steamy bathroom or kept well watered in a frost-free greenhouse.
- Chinese water chestnut (*Eleocharis dulcis* 'Variegate'), a tender marginal plant which resembles a variegated rush and requires a planting depth of 15cm (6in).

1 Place each of the marginal plants in a plastic pot large enough to allow plenty of room for growth. Fill each one with loam or compost, leaving about 3cm (1¼in) at the top for a mulch of aquatic gravel. The roots of aquatic plants get tangled together very easily, so keep each one in a polythene bag before planting. This also prevents damage through drying out.

2 Arrange the pots on dry land to make a pleasing composition. Fill the container with fresh water. Wearing rubber gloves, position the tallest plant, using bricks to achieve the optimum depth.

3 Add the rest of the pots, then fill in the gaps with floating aquatic plants.

4 Tall reeds, bamboos and rushes planted in pots need shelter from wind because their roots will not give the same stability as if they were planted directly into the soil. They all thrive in good light, but need protection from continuous hot sun, which will overheat the water.

VARIATION

For a dramatic effect at night, place an underwater light at the bottom of the container. A low-voltage halogen light is the safest and very effective. It must be connected to a socket indoors and protected by an approved circuit-breaker.

BUBBLE FOUNTAIN

Moving water and crushed glass are used to create a sparkling feature suitable for a limited space. The fountain springs up from a hole in the ground and trickles over large slate paddle stones, surrounded by 'ripples' of crushed glass and rings of smaller stones.

A small submersible pump will give spray heights of 30–90cm (12–36in), the highest of which only requires a pond diameter of 90cm (36in). The electrically powered pump is neat, quiet and easy to install; it should be connected to a socket indoors and protected by a circuit-breaker. The fountain is relatively maintenance-free, but the reservoir must never be allowed to run dry or the pump will burn out. The pump should not be operated or left outside in freezing conditions.

This water feature is not suitable in a garden with young children.

MATERIALS AND TOOLS

- 20kg (45lb) fine sand
- butyl lining
- clean new brick
- submersible pump, with cable
- rigid wire mesh (as used for animal and bird cages)
- wire-cutters
- conduit for the pump cable and circuit-breaker
- 60kg (132lb) of 10–15cm (4–6in) slate paddle stones (produced industrially in tumbling machines)
- 40kg (88lb) of 1cm (½in) clear crushed glass
- 60kg (132lb) of 1cm (½in) green crushed glass

Left: Commercially produced crushed glass, originally developed for aquariums, is wonderful when used as a garden mulch and within water features. It is quite safe for both plants and fish and is available in different colours and sizes.

1 Choose a site away from falling leaves. Dig a hole deep enough to submerge the entire pump when it is standing on the brick. Excavate the sides to a diameter of 90–120cm (3–4ft), with a fall towards the central reservoir. Discard any loose stones and, unless the topsoil is very fine, cover the area with a layer of sand.

2 Place the lining in the hole, flattening it at the bottom, then pleat it in flat folds as it extends out of the hole. Leave the excess hanging over the edge. Place the brick in the hole with the pump on top. Make sure it is steady and level. Place the wire mesh centrally over the hole and, using wire-cutters, cut out a small circle large enough for the pump stem to protrude through. Lay the cable generously over the lining until it reaches the edge then feed it through the conduit, ideally buried out of sight, to the electrical source.

*Right: The huge leaves of the giant prickly rhubarb (*Gunnera manicata*) growing behind the bubble fountain give a sense of mystery. These water-loving plants grow well in rich, moist bog garden soil.*

3 Flood the excavated area with water, ensuring that the reservoir is completely full. Test the pump and adjust the flow if necessary. While the pump is running, arrange the largest paddle stones in a natural-looking ring. Make a thick mound of clear crushed glass around the stones, so that half are submerged and half are above the surface but glistening with spray. Add a ring of smaller stones, then a sloping mound of green crushed glass shaped like a gentle ripple. Conceal the edge with a ring of small Paddlestones. Trim the lining so that it is concealed under the stones.

decorating with plants

In many traditional gardens it is the plants, trees and shrubs that create the design and atmosphere but some outside spaces can employ plants to emphasize a style or perform a specific function. A single tree or tropical palm can create a focal point, a raised bed filled with culinary herbs will provide constant fresh flavourings, and an evergreen climber can be used as a contrasting colour that will enhance the tone and texture of a wall or trellis.

LEFT The perfectly symmetrical architectural form of the agave plant provides a strong sculptural plant in frost-free spaces.

Above: This sun-baked courtyard is an outside space that relies entirely on container-grown plants to create borders of lush, aromatic and drought-tolerant plants. They are planted in similar terracotta pots.

In outdoor spaces that are primarily designed for people, plants may need to fulfil a specific role as well as being purely decorative. Before you select each plant, it is a useful discipline to determine its contribution to your outside space before thinking of its appearance. Containers are invaluable, particularly in a small space, because they enable you to move shapes, colours and textures around to create different effects.

Successful gardening also depends on accurately analysing the site so that you can choose plants that will be happy growing there. You can improve the soil and control the watering, but it is impossible to completely change the local climate. For a plant to be strong and healthy, it needs to be grown in a place that is as close as possible to its natural habitat.

Some of the most successful contemporary gardens contain only three or four different types of plant, complementing the simplicity of modern interiors. Having a clear idea of the style of outdoor space you wish to create will help you to formulate a shortlist of 'must-have' plants. By a careful process of elimination, you can then narrow down the choice to find the right plant for any given position.

The right plant in the right place

A plant's natural environment is the main clue to its ideal planting position. Plants that would normally grow under trees are likely to thrive in a garden shaded by high walls and surrounding buildings, while plants that flourish in hot, windy coastal areas stand the best chance of tolerating the arid conditions found on exposed urban roof terraces. Even in the smallest space there will probably be some variation of light and shade, to which different plants will be suited.

If you want to grow a climber over an outside wall, a south- or west-facing wall is far preferable to one facing north or east, which will inevitably be colder and receive significantly less sun. Some climbers require no support, but others will need a trellis or an invisible framework of wires to scramble up. A wall will also be improved by a range of shrubs and trees that can be trained and pruned against it; tall, narrow shapes look particularly elegant. Shrubs with sharp thorns and impenetrable foliage provide security against intruders, and others offer summer scent and flowers at a time of the year when you are most likely to be outside.

Dedicated cooks may want to devote their available space to edible plants which, with careful planning, will provide home-grown produce for most of the year. Growing your own herbs is particularly satisfying and economical as most of them require very little space and frequent picking stimulates more generous growth. Mixing ornamental flowers with salad leaves and vegetables is an attractive way to combine the practical with the decorative, and certain kinds of companion planting will deter destructive insects and encourage pollinating bees.

Left: The perimeter is the strongest part of this roof terrace. Specially-made lightweight containers soften the hard edges of the safety barrier and also provide a degree of privacy.

Above: Edible plants like kale, chard and the riotous nasturtiums may be intermingled with more decorative plants, particularly those that deter unwanted destructive insects.

Designing with colour

Flowers and leaves have inspiring scents and shapes, but the initial impact from a garden or outdoor space is usually one of colour. Most flowers and deciduous shrubs and trees are short-lived, temporarily changing the permanent colour scheme of walls, floor surfaces, outdoor furniture and evergreens. Even evergreen is not one colour, but a whole range of shades and tones to add to your palette. A successful exterior colour scheme is thus a subtle relationship between nature and the fabricated elements. The architecture of an adjoining building and the tone and texture of the exterior woodwork and masonry are essential ingredients in an outside colour scheme. Some of these elements are fixed, but by painting a wall or trellis, or adding a different floor covering or style of furniture, you can add a permanent colour that will enhance the colours around it.

Below: The red buds and pink flowers of primula vialii *are short-lived, but they still make a spectacular display for a few weeks in summer. An ideal candidate for a large container.*

As for the flowers and foliage, it is a misguided notion that all plant combinations are pleasing. In the wild, flowers and plants tend to create their own natural harmony, but many of the modified colours of cultivated hybrids are not what nature intended. Exotic imported plants look attractive in a garden centre but they do not always integrate happily into our climate. If in doubt, remember that plants that naturally grow together are more likely to create a pleasing effect.

The quality and quantity of natural light has a dramatic effect on how we perceive colours. An outside space that makes the most of the changing light throughout the day will give added dimension to the colours within it. Hot, flame colours zing out in the midday sun but are lost in the evening shadows, when blues and purples radiate a subtle luminescence, as do all shades of white, silver and cream. Strong, bright colours are perfect against the brilliant blue sky in countries such as Greece, where dazzling whitewashed walls, acid lime green painted timber and vibrant pink bougainvilleas are an exciting combination, but they lose their impact in the softer, slanting light of northern countries, which is more sympathetic to subtle pastel tones. Daylight varies enormously depending on the time of day and the season, and the amount of shade also determines the effect of different colours.

Left: Plants are visually more effective when placed and repeated in large blocks. Their flowers and foliage combined make a greater impact on sight and their colours, textures and hues create a harmonious effect.

Above: The use of old fruit boxes provides planters with a nautical theme for a roof terrace. This can be emphasized by using fleshy leaved sedum, wispy grasses and shingle mulch.

Creating an instant effect

A new garden, traditionally planted, will take several years to reach maturity, but an outside room can include some judicious cheating to realize a finished result much sooner. Buying mature plants and trees is a major purchase, but worthwhile if you consider that you are paying for the years a nursery or specialist grower has taken to raise and tend them. Specialists may also be able to offer expert advice on the most suitable species for your space and location. A single ten-year-old tree would make an impressive focal point on a paved terrace, while a tall thicket of lush bamboo would create instant shade and shelter around a seating area.

Many trees and shrubs will thrive quite happily in containers, and you have the option of taking them with you if you move house. To do well in pots, plants need either to be slow-growing by nature, or pruned to maintain a balance between the size of the roots and the amount of foliage. Hardy exotics such as palms, phormium and fatsia are slow-growing, whereas bay (*Laurus nobilis*), olive (*Olea europaea*), common box (*Buxus sempervirens*) and the strawberry tree (*Arbutus unedo*) can be clipped into distinctive shapes – balls, pyramids, mopheads and lollipops. These topiary shapes restrict the plants' size at the same time as giving them a strong, attractive outline. Other plants, including the many varieties of grasses and bamboo, have such invasive root systems that they are better off contained in pots.

Containers have maximum flexibility in that they are reasonably easy to move. If you are at all uncertain about the designing of your gardening scheme, it is a great advantage to be able to look at individual plants in the context of

Left: The curvaceous contours of gigantic pots illustrate the importance of selecting containers for their aesthetic merit and not just as vessels to hold plants. Used singly or grouped together, they contribute to outside decoration and style.

other features in the outdoor space, and to be able to move them into different positions and configurations. Containers allow experimentation.

It is almost impossible to choose a container that is too big for a space, and one huge pot will look far more impressive than scores of little ones. Another advantage of buying big is that, even left unplanted, a beautiful large amphora or curvaceous urn has the dramatic presence of a sculpture. Place it at a focal point, in a corner to soften hard vertical lines, or at the end of a path to create a vista. The extra space afforded by a large container allows you to grow masses of the same plant for greater impact, or to grow one tall permanent tree or shrub. If you opt for the latter, you can still provide seasonal interest by underplanting with bulbs and annuals. Remember that big, in the context of containers, can be beautiful, but will also be heavy.

The value of contained spaces

Container gardening is not only about growing plants in pots, it can also be perceived as planting in contained spaces such as a raised bed, a narrow strip between a wall and paving, crevices among stones and slabs, a water feature or a gravelled area. A great advantage of contained gardening is that the level of maintenance can be manipulated. In a contained area the soil quality can easily be improved, watering is more localized, and the type and density of planting can be controlled.

The height of a raised bed will dramatically change the scale and proportions of a small space. If you incorporate seating alongside the bed, the plants will feel closer and more intimate, an effect that is enhanced if you grow scented varieties. Raised areas lend themselves to strategic seasonal planting. For example, in early spring you could look out across a raised bed to view the whole of the space beyond, whereas later in the year you could create a living screen of tall plants that will divide one part of the garden from another. Fast-growing annuals such as fennel (*Foeniculum vulgare*) and sunflowers (*Helianthus annus*) reach well over 2m (6ft) in a couple of months, as do perennials such as *Verbena bonariensis* and meadow rue (*Thalictrum rochebruneanum*), which should then be cut back in the winter. Raised beds can also offer numerous advantages to the vegetable gardener. They are far less backbreaking to tend, and many of the pests that plague edibles at ground level such as carrot fly, slugs and snails, are far easier to control organically on a contained, higher level.

If you have a narrow space between a wall and paving, this is an ideal position for a single-layer climber, which you can easily keep well trained. Mulch the ground at its feet with a thick layer of stones or gravel, using a colour to blend with the colour of the paving, and this will prevent water evaporation and suppress weeds. If you deliberately leave sufficient space when laying paving stones on a terrace, small alpines or mat-forming plants will colonize very freely.

In a gravel garden, pots may be concealed in deep planting pockets covered by stones, making the plants easier to move or divide when they outgrow their individual containers. The

Above: Combining plants successfully takes as much skill as fusing food flavours or co-ordinating colours. A perfect union is the vibrant agapanthus *and the skeletal* eryngium.

same principle may be applied to water features, where plants considered to be invasive are held in check by keeping them contained in pots, partially or completely submerged in the water. As with dry land container gardening, plants can be grouped together and rearranged when one fades and another reaches its prime.

Roof Terraces

Weight is an important consideration on roof terraces and balconies. Ask a structural engineer or architect to calculate weight-loading capacity, which will depend on the number and size of beams in the roof or the balcony's structure. The edge of a roof is the strongest part, so the ideal planting solution is a container that runs around the perimeter. This will also create a solid safety barrier if the roof is enclosed by railings rather than a wall. The back of the container could provide a fixing point for a screen of trellis, on which climbing plants would give shelter and privacy. If the roof has a timber deck, a wooden planter made from the same flooring material would fit in well. Wind is usually a problem on roof gardens, so unless the space is completely sheltered, it is vital to create a windbreak. Choose plants with tough foliage or those that are small and compact, and will not be ruffled by gusts and gales. Remember that however drought- and wind-resistant your choice of planting, it is untenable to consider rooftop gardening without an easily accessible source of water.

Whether at roof level or on the ground, contained and container plants cannot develop deep enough root systems to survive prolonged spells of drought. Contained gardening is therefore high maintenance, but there are likely to be considerably fewer plants than in a traditional garden so it may be viable to install an automatic watering and feeding system. Watering by hand, however, can be very satisfying, and is only usually necessary when the weather makes you want to be in the fresh air enjoying your outside space.

Left: An Aegean blue stained wood window box complements the subtle greens of flowering echeveria *and bluey-grey* Agave americana.

Below: On a rooftop, the tall galvanised containers complement the lead flashings. The grey Festuca glauca *resembles billowing smoke.*

DECORATED POTS

Most perennial herbs, particularly those Mediterranean natives that flourish in a well-drained light soil and a sheltered, sunny position, are ideal candidates for container gardening. Woody-stemmed herbs like lavender may be trained as decorative topiary balls and the silvery grey-green foliage is enhanced by painting clay Long Toms in a pale pistachio-coloured emulsion with a broad white band to highlight a white gravel mulch.

MATERIALS AND TOOLS

- 3 clay or pale terracotta pots
- pale green water-based emulsion paint
- white acrylic paint
- soil-based potting compost
- 3 pot-grown lavender plants
- white pea gravel
- metal tray
- paintbrush
- masking tape

1 Brush off any loose material on the pots and ensure the surface is dry. Paint the outside and top few inches inside the pot with a generous layer of pale green paint. Leave the pots to dry for at least 24 hours in a cool well-aired place. Mask off an area under the rim approximately 2.5cm (1in) wide. Paint the strip you have masked off with the white acrylic paint. Using short pieces of overlapping tape helps to keep the edges of the band straight and parallel.

2 Remove the pieces of tape very carefully when the paint is completely dry. Plant the lavender, leaving space at the top of each pot for a generous layer of pea-gravel mulch. Add a layer of gravel to the metal tray, and place the pots on top.

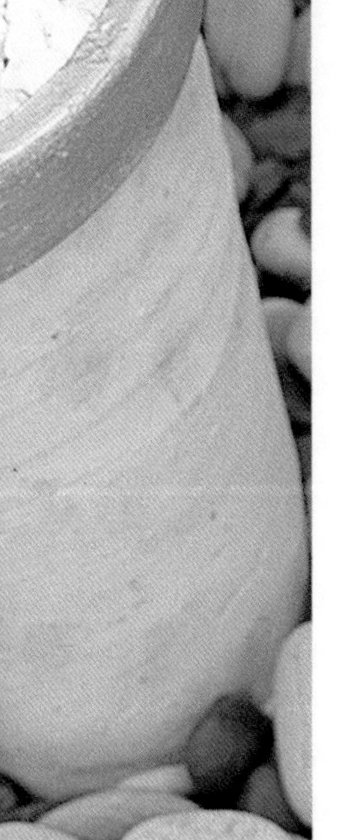

Above: Light, protective gloves should always be worn when applying gilding material.

VARIATIONS

A burnished effect around the rim can be created by using a gilding material with a wax base.

Sea shells and smooth rounded beach pebbles make an alternative mulch.

Other suitable plants include topiarized rosemary bushes, which would also be useful for culinary purposes.

VARIATIONS

Above: A metal container may be customized using the same masking technique as the painted pots by using metallic or car spray paint.

Right: The colour and shape of these *Bellis perennis* (English daisy) flowers is repeated on the painted terracotta pot with the addition of a flat white shell, glued in place with waterproof adhesive.

TWO-TIER CONTAINER

If space is at a premium it is vital to make the most of it, vertically and horizontally. For example, a large square or rectangular container will fit snugly into the corner of a balcony and provide more room for plants than a collection of small circular pots.

A two-tier container gives the opportunity for temporary planting in the top tier, which can be changed each season without disrupting the permanent display below. The top tier can be considered rather like a vase, in which plants are replaced regularly after flowering. Scented plants such as lilies and nicotiana, whose perfume increases after dusk, are especially welcome in a small space. Another attractive idea is to grow perennial herbs in the bottom tier, with annual herbs such as chervil or basil in the top. You could also grow acid-loving plants in one tier, and plants that prefer alkaline conditions below.

Right: The oyster shell mulch helps to retain the moist environment that fragrant lily-of-the-valley (Convallaria majalis) *prefer.*

Right: Glass panels set into the metal barrier protect flowers and foliage from the desiccating effect of wind that is most plants' worst enemy.

MATERIALS AND EQUIPMENT

- 2 different-sized stainless steel or galvanized containers, in similar style
- metal punch
- coarse grit
- bricks (optional)
- good-quality sterile potting compost
- selection of permanent plants, e.g. lacecap hydrangea (*Hydrangea macrophylla*) and variegated ivy (*Hedera helix*), and temporary plants, e.g. lily-of-the-valley (*Convallaria majalis*)
- oyster shells

1 Containers dry out in warm weather but they can also become waterlogged, which will make the roots of the plants rot. Pierce several rows of small holes in the base of the large container. Spread a thick layer of coarse grit in the bottom to allow excess water to drain away.

2 It is easier to position the smaller top container before planting up the lower tier. Depending on the height of the plants in the top tier, you may want to raise the small container on a couple of bricks.

3 Fill both containers with compost. Plant the hydrangea and ivy in the lower tier, then plant the lily-of-the-valley in the top. Cover the compost with a layer of oyster shells as a decorative mulch.

4 A two-tier container filled with plants and soil is very difficult to move without dismantling it. One solution is to place your container on a small mobile platform, preferably with braked casters. This is extremely useful when you want to move it in and out of the shade in hot weather.

5 In winter, the rootballs of container-grown plants may need to be insulated. Line the inside of each container with pieces of thin polystyrene sheet, or wrap the outside with several layers of hessian tied in place with string. In severe weather, a layer of bubble-wrap plastic underneath the hessian will provide additional insulation.

RAISED BAMBOO BED

The easiest way to change the level in an outside area is with a raised bed. This can divide the space into smaller compartments, or provide a base for dense planting to disguise a boundary. A permanent bed can be made from frost-proof bricks, but here a temporary raised bed has been constructed using a timber box frame with bamboo panels. This will hide a mismatched collection of pots or plastic growbags, and grouping plants closely together makes watering easier and also helps prevent evaporation in hot weather. Inside the box frame the pots or growbags can be raised to the same level on bricks, which will also deter slugs and snails. The softwood frame is coated with a combined wood preservative/stain, chosen to enhance the subtle colours of the rosemary and sage flowers. The corners are constructed with butt joints, so it requires only the most basic carpentry skills.

MATERIALS AND TOOLS

to make a box frame 50cm x 1m (19½ x 39in)

- 4 each of the following lengths of 5 x 2.5cm (2 x 1in) planed softwood: 1m (39in), 31cm (12in), 45cm (18in)
- hammer
- corrugated fasteners
- drill
- 5cm (2in) galvanized screws
- screwdriver
- waterproof woodfiller
- fine-grade sandpaper
- coloured woodstain/preservative
- decorator's paintbrush
- 20 bamboo poles, 1m (39in) long
- hacksaw
- galvanized veneer pins

Left: Several varieties of mint, rosemary and sage, planted in individual pots, create the impression of a lush herb garden surrounded by the 'sleeve' of a timber and bamboo fence.

1 Construct two sides of the box frame, using two 1m (39in) and two 31cm (12in) lengths of timber. On all four sides, hammer through two corrugated fasteners, catching both pieces of timber to make a perfect right angle. Repeat to make the other side of the frame.

2 Drill two holes at each end of both halves of the frame then screw on a 45cm (18in) length of timber to form a crosspiece. Repeat with the other three 45cm (18in) lengths to make the box shape. Conceal the screwheads with woodfiller, then rub smooth with sandpaper.

3 Paint the frame inside and out with wood preservative/stain and leave to dry. Cut the bamboo into 35cm (14in) lengths, using a hacksaw. (Bamboo tends to splinter so a fine-toothed blade will give a much cleaner cut.) Pin the bamboo round the inside of the frame, using veneer pins.

outdoor eating

Eating in the fresh air is quite a different experience to having a meal indoors. Al fresco diners seem to lose track of time and often a summer lunch lingers on long after the sun has gone down. Enjoying the simple pleasure of home-grown food or the smokey flavours of a barbecue can become an addictive pleasure. Simplicity is the key to such relaxed and memorable occasions.

LEFT A single sprig of garden-grown lavender adds a tiny but very sensitive personal touch to this simply dressed table.

Above: This is a simple kitchen with the merest basics for outdoor eating and food preparation. It is decorated in the warm and sunny colours of the Mediterranean.

Eating al fresco has to be one of life's greatest pleasures. The best and most memorable outdoor meals are usually the simplest – freshly brewed coffee with warm croissants, a sandwich stuffed with crispy salad and a sharp-flavoured cheese, or just-caught, well-seasoned fish hot off the barbecue. The fresh air sharpens the appetite and eating with your hands is a sensual and satisfying experience.

Grilling food over an open fire is the most basic form of outdoor cooking, although it requires some practice to perfect this primeval skill. Some of the finest outdoor food can be cooked merely on a raised metal grill over burning coals, and the secret of success is keeping the recipes simple. If you assemble all the ingredients in advance, this kind of cooking can become an addictive pleasure but, however well organised you are, there is always the unpredictable element of the weather. Unlike gas or electricity a wood or charcoal fire will be drastically affected by a strong wind, a damp atmosphere or even the ambient temperature. There are barbecues fuelled by gas or electricity, which guarantee successful results every time, but they tend to be bulky and rather ugly.

Outdoor cooking need not be restricted to grilling. The same grill or barbecue can be used to make single-pan dishes such as Spanish paella or a fish stew flavoured with hot spices, or with fresh ginger and lemongrass. If you prefer to cook in the comfort of your own kitchen, you can carry hot dishes outside and place them on basic plate-warmers heated by nightlights, the sort you often see in Indian restaurants. If you are entertaining in the evening, it is essential to have good overhead lighting to illuminate any steps or paths you may have to negotiate while carrying a hot tureen or tray of glasses.

The outdoor kitchen

It would be inconceivable to design a home without a kitchen, yet many outside spaces are created without even considering the possibility of a place to cook. If a barbecue is being purpose-built in an outside space, it can be designed following the principles of good kitchen design. Ideally, the hob area will be enclosed by two heat-resistant worktops at approximately hip height, which feel comfortable to work at – barbecuing for a party can be a lengthy affair. If the grill is at waist level, there will be room underneath for storing charcoal or wood chips.

As well as the cooking area you need a work surface large enough to take several plates of prepared food ready for cooking. Space should be made for the cooked food, preferably on the other side of the grill. Separating these surfaces avoids the danger of putting cooked food on a plate that has previously held raw meat or fish, which could result in food poisoning.

Above: Once the doors to this kitchen are rolled back, the transition between inside and outside is invisible. The open-shelving becomes an elegant and practical sideboard.

If al fresco barbecues are to be held in the evening, it is essential to provide adequate lighting to cook by and so that your guests can see what they are eating. The grill or barbecue will emit some light, but it is impossible to see clearly whether food is cooked without some form of overhead illumination. Provided there is space, a sink with running water is useful. It means that all the food preparation can be done outdoors, particularly those messy jobs such as cleaning and gutting fish, washing vegetables and herbs, and cleaning the barbecue after use.

Within easy reach of the outdoor cook should be a basic batterie de cuisine. A basting brush will apply oil or glaze as the food cooks, long-handled tongs with a comfortable grip and firm jaws are used to turn items on the grill, and a flexible metal fish slice will lift off the food once it is cooked. Fish-shaped metal baskets allow you to turn grilling fish without any danger of them breaking up, and similar square or oblong baskets can be used for cooking vegetables. Insulated gauntlets are should be used during cooking and for cleaning the grill afterwards.

A permanent outdoor area with solid worktops made of heatproof and waterproof materials and with access to running water can be extremely versatile. You can use it for practical gardening tasks such as potting, planting and sowing seeds, and for buffet-style entertaining.

Cooking al fresco

Barbecuing is simple in essence, but in practice it is the most difficult method of cooking perfectly. Once you have cooked regularly on the same barbecue using the same-quality charcoal, you quickly develop the instinct of knowing exactly when to start putting food on the grill and how long it will take to cook. Modern barbecues are designed to take the guesswork out of heat control, but a bed of glowing charcoal is more difficult to work with. There are no temperature controls on a charcoal barbecue, and that is part of the challenge. It may be great for searing a steak but could completely incinerate the delicate flesh of a fish. Judging when charcoal is fit to cook over can only really be determined by feel and sight.

If you are cooking in daylight, the coals are ready when there are no flames and they have turned grey and started to look powdery. After dark, it is easier to see when there is no flicker of a flame and the coals emit a consistent red glow. When it is impossible to hold your hand over the charcoals for more than a second, the temperature is hot enough to brown the outside of meat but leave the inside rare. Charcoal cooking requires constant attention, and you should never leave open flames unattended.

More control, and therefore more consistent success, can be achieved with a modern barbecue. Cheap, disposable barbecues consist of a self-contained pack containing a heavy foil tray, charcoal and a wire grid. You have no choice but to wait until the charcoal reaches the optimum temperature before starting to cook. This kind of barbecue will usually burn for about 2 hours and is big enough to cook food for two or three people. Larger, kettle-style barbecues and those built into a stone or brick wall can be fitted with movable grills and adjusted so that they are closer or farther away from the charcoal. The wider area also allows space to spread out the coals and distribute the heat. This can be

lowered, to an indeterminate degree, by a squirt of water from a spray bottle. A water spray close at hand is an excellent way of dealing with any actual flames, should they appear.

An important safety precaution is never to position a barbecue close to buildings, wooden fences, plants or overhanging trees, which could easily get scorched. A strong wind will cause the coals to burn faster and hotter, and gusting winds will create drifting clouds of smoke. A covered barbecue has distinct advantages here, particularly if it has a ventilated lid offering protection from both wind and rain. Barbecues are synonymous with hot summer days and balmy evenings, but there is also something very appealing about cooking outside on a crisp winter's night, serving roasted chestnuts and spicy sausages with mugs of piping hot soup. Potatoes with well-scrubbed skins can be wrapped in foil and cooked in the embers, campfire style. Resist the urge to put too much meat on a barbecue as the fat will drip onto the coals and you will be enveloped in a cloud of smoke, unpleasant for you and your guests, not to mention your neighbours.

From an environmental point of view, it is worth searching out locally produced charcoal derived from coppicing, a wildlife-friendly practice that benefits many species, including bluebells, nightingales and dormice. As an alternative to charcoal, specialist barbecue stores often stock a range of woods such as apple, oak and mesquite, a wood indigenous to North America and claimed by many to be the finest fuel for barbecuing.

Left: The Zen-inspired oak and steel furniture is offset by warm iroko decking and ochre-coloured walls. This creates an intimate dining and cooking area.

The perfect occasion

The secret of successful entertaining is good planning. An outdoor meal is normally leisurely, and the joy of the occasion is its relaxed informality. Aim to prepare all the food in advance and consider presentation as well as content. In countries where outdoor eating is commonplace, most of the dishes are put on the table at the outset within easy reach of the guests.

All that is needed for a delicious cold meal is a savoury tart with seasonal salads, dressed at the last minute, some fine cheeses and wine, and plenty of fresh fruit. If you are cooking on a grill or barbecue, most meat and oily fish such as sardines, anchovies, mackerel and herring need nothing more than seasoning and a light brushing of olive oil. Vegetables such as tomatoes, mushrooms, peppers, onions and fennel benefit from a simple marinade of fresh lemon juice, herbs, extra-virgin olive oil and honey, while sweetcorn is best barbecued in its own protective husk. In Indonesia a popular method of grilling fish is to wrap it in banana leaves, which adds to the flavour although the banana leaves themselves are not edible. Vine leaves from the garden or supermarket can be used in the same way and are edible.

Left: A table shaded by a sail cloth canopy makes a perfect setting for all day dining. Paraffin lamps add a romantic touch as evening falls.

Below: This galvanised metal barbecue is lightweight and easily transportable, requiring a minimal amount of charcoal; perfect for an inpromptu meal for two.

Kebabs are very popular at barbecues but need to be prepared in advance as the process of threading onto skewers is time-consuming. The ingredients for each kebab should have a similar cooking time and be cut to a uniform size, large enough to hold their shape during cooking. Soaking wooden skewers in water overnight will prevent them burning, and pre-oiling metal skewers will stop the cooked food from sticking.

The difference between a pleasant meal and a really memorable occasion are the finishing touches that make you and your guests feel at ease. If the meal is likely to be a long affair, make sure that the seating is comfortable. Fast-food restaurants reputedly design their seats to become uncomfortable very quickly, and weatherproof outdoor furniture may have the same effect unless the seats and backs are insulated with a layer of cushioning. Remember also that eating with your fingers is fun and relaxing, especially if you have provided enough napkins and finger bowls within easy reach. As you can never predict exactly when barbecue food will be ready, ensure that you provide plenty of tasty snacks, salads and breads as the aroma from the grill combined with the open air will inevitably sharpen people's appetites.

ENTERTAINING OUTDOORS

Entertaining al fresco is a wonderful way to share your outside room with family and friends. Choose dishes to suit the season – simple salads, soft, summer fruits and thirst-quenching drinks for hot days and firm-fleshed fish and seafood cooked over an aromatic barbecue. Prepare as much as possible in advance so you can enjoy and share the experience.

QUAIL'S EGGS AND CHERRY TOMATOES ON CRESS

Even if you do not have a garden, it is easy to grow mustard and cress. The tiny seeds take 3 or 4 days to germinate and grow into a grassy base for this attractive dish.

INGREDIENTS

- quails' eggs and cherry tomatoes
- white paper kitchen towel
- large plate with a flat bottom and raised rim
- packet of mustard and cress seeds
- clear plastic film
- water spray

1 Cut the kitchen towel to fit the flat part of the plate. Soak it with fresh, cold water then sprinkle the seeds evenly over the top. Cover the plate with plastic film and place in a warm, dark place.

2 When the seeds have germinated, usually 24–48 hours, remove the film and put the plate near a window with good light. Spray the seeds regularly with water to keep the kitchen towel moist.

3 Hard-boil the quail's eggs and remove the shells. Place the mustard and cress on a serving dish and arrange the quail's eggs and cherry tomatoes in little groups on top.

BARBECUED PRAWNS

Prawns are the simplest food to barbecue. They take only minutes to cook and are delicious eaten piping hot, dipped in home-made mayonnaise, a tangy salsa or a spicy peanut sauce. Cooking them on a bed of lemon or lime slices stops the prawns from sticking to the grill, making them easier to turn over.

INGREDIENTS

- barbecue and charcoal
- sprigs of rosemary, lavender or fennel
- fresh raw large or tiger prawns
- wooden skewers, soaked overnight in water
- lemons or limes

1 Light the barbecue well in advance. When all the flames have disappeared, add sprigs of rosemary, lavender or fennel to create aromatic smoke and deter insects.

2 Meanwhile remove the heads and shells of the prawns, and the black vein which runs down the back. Wash them in plenty of cold water.

3 Thread each prawn onto two wooden skewers. Place a layer of lemon or lime slices on the barbecue grill and lay the prawns on top. Turn over the skewers after about 2 minutes. The prawns are cooked when they are pale pink with browned edges. Eat immediately.

ICED BOWLS

These beautiful ice sculptures are very simple to make, and will create an impressive centrepiece for a summer party or special occasion. They melt rapidly but will hold their shape long enough for you to serve home-made ice-cream or sorbet in the centre.

If you have flowers in bloom, iced bowls cost absolutely nothing other than your time. Start making them 2 days before you need them.

1 Put a layer of crushed ice in the larger glass bowl. Place the smaller bowl on top, and fill it with marbles or pebbles to weight it down and hold it in place.

2 Fill the gap between the two bowls with a layer of ice, followed by a layer of flowers. Repeat with more alternating layers until you reach the top. Pour in enough chilled water to fill the gaps and up to the top. Freeze for 24 hours.

3 Remove the marbles or pebbles and fill the inside with tepid water, which will release the inner glass bowl. Dip the outer glass bowl in a sink of tepid water until the iced bowl can be gently swivelled away. Return to the freezer.

MATERIALS AND TOOLS

- crushed ice cubes
- 2 similar-shaped freezer-proof glass bowls, one smaller than the other
- marbles or pebbles
- several handfuls of brightly coloured flowerheads
- jug of chilled water

SUMMER FRUIT JELLY

A cake, brioche or loaf tin makes an excellent jelly mould because metal is the best conductor of heat, which makes it easy to remove the jelly. Freezer-proof, rigid plastic boxes give more contemporary geometric shapes.

Use whole seasonal fruits or large slices. Avoid fresh pineapple and papaya as these contain an enzyme that breaks down gelatine, and the jelly will refuse to set.

1 Make up the gelatine mixture following the packet instructions but substituting grape juice for water. Use enough gelatine to make a firm jelly.

2 Layer the fruits generously in the mould, packing them firmly around the sides. Pour over the cooled jelly liquid and refrigerate until completely set.

3 Stand the mould for 20 seconds in a bowl of hot water until the sides of the jelly begin to melt, then invert on to a flat plate. If the jelly does not move, give the mould a firm shake in case there is a vacuum in the top of the mould. Keep the jelly in the refrigerator until ready to serve.

INGREDIENTS

- gelatine leaf or powdered gelatine
- white grape juice
- selection of fresh fruit, e.g. peaches, nectarines, strawberries, raspberries, blackberries and redcurrants
- jellymould

PICKLED CHERRIES

This savoury hors d'oeuvre, very popular in the South of France, is inspired by a Jane Grigson recipe. It is a wonderful way to use cherries, which have a short but plentiful season. The cherries make a delicious alternative to olives. They take about a month to mature but can be eaten after 2 weeks.

INGREDIENTS

- 1kg (2.2lb) ripe, firm cherries
- clean, dry preserving jars or plastic-lidded jam jars
- 1 litre (2 pints) white wine vinegar
- 600g (1¼lb) granulated sugar
- 6 cloves, crushed
- 4 juniper berries, crushed
- zest of 2 lemons
- 2cm (¾in) stick of cinnamon

1 Rinse and dry the cherries, discarding any damaged fruit. Cut the stalks down to about 1cm (½in) and pack the fruit tightly into the jars.

2 Bring the remaining ingredients to the boil in a stainless steel or enamelled pan, then simmer for 10 minutes. Leave overnight.

3 Remove the cinnamon stick and pour the liquid over the cherries until they are well covered. Store in a dark, cool, dry cupboard.

ICED TEAS

Quench summer thirsts by serving these lightly scented teas, which complement barbecued food and fruity desserts. Lemongrass and mint tea is also delicious served hot with Thai or Chinese food.

INGREDIENTS

For peach tea

- finest Ceylon tea leaves
- ripe peach

For lemongrass and mint tea

- lemongrass stalks
- fresh mint leaves
- extra sprigs of fresh mint

1 To make a peach-flavoured tea, infuse the tea leaves with enough boiling water to make a weak tea. Allow to cool. Cut the peach and remove the stone, slice the flesh, add to the tea, and chill.

2 To make lemongrass and mint tea, slice the lemongrass stalks into rounds. Put in a heatproof jug with the mint leaves and boiling water. Cool, then chill. Remove the mint leaves and add a few sprigs of fresh mint for decoration.

BURNING LAVENDER STICKS

Lavender is renowned as an insect repellent and its essential oil is very soothing for insect bites. When burning, lavender releases a pleasant scent but one unattractive to gnats and mosquitoes. The sticks burn very quickly so make plenty to last the evening. Stick three or four lavender sticks in an incense burner or improvise by using a bowl filled with sand.

As with lighted candles, never leave the burning sticks unattended.

MATERIALS AND TOOLS

- dried lavender
- saltpetre (potassium nitrate), available from herbalists and aromatherapy suppliers

1 Soak the flowerheads and upper stalks of the lavender in a solution of 1 cup warm water and 2 tablespoons saltpetre. Leave for at least an hour.

2 Remove the lavender from the solution. Tie the stalks in a bunch and hang upside down to dry.

If you are particularly attractive to gnats and mosquitoes, you can protect yourself further by making a sweet-smelling and moisturising oil. Mix 2 drops each of lavender and lemongrass essential oils with 10ml of grapeseed or sweet almond oil. Rub gently onto vulnerable areas such as ankles and wrists.

SOURCES AND MATERIALS

Architectural Plants
Nuthurst, Horsham
West Sussex RH13 6LH
tel: 01403 891772
(big, bold hardy exotics)

Barbary Pots
45 Fernshaw Road
London SW10 0TN
tel: 020 7352 1053
(pale Moroccan terracotta pots)

Capital Garden Products
Gibbs Reed Barn
Pashley Road, Ticehurst
East Sussex TN5 7HE
tel: 01580 201092
(fibreglass and resin with authentic-looking metal and terracotta finishes)

The Conran Shop
Michelin House
81 Fulham Road
London SW3 6RD
tel: 020 7589 7401
(contemporary designs – also furniture and accessories)

Deltalight (UK)
Crown House
Lower Street, Haslemere
Surrey GU27 2PD
tel: 01428 651919
(contemporary lighting manufacturer)

Henry Doubleday Research Association (HDRA)
Ryton Organic Gardens
Coventry
Warwickshire CV8 3LG
tel: 01203 303517

S & B Evans & Sons
7A Ezra Street
London E2 7RH
tel: 020 7729 6635
(hand-thrown terracotta and glazed garden pots, water features)

Festival International des Jardins
Ferme du Château
41150 Chaumont-sur-Loire
France
tel: 00 33 254 209922
(innovative garden design festival, 185km south of Paris, from mid June–mid October)

Hotspot Heaters
Cricket St Thomas Estate Office
Chard
Somerset TA20 4DB
tel: 01460 30600

Jonathan Garratt
Hare Lane Pottery
Cranborne
Wimborne
Dorset BH21 5QT
tel: 01725 517700
(wood-fired hand-thrown pots African and Eastern designs)

Garden Heritage
Manor Road Nursery
Manor Road
Milford-on-Sea
Lymington
Hampshire SO41 0RG
tel: 01590 644888
(Japanese garden collection of features, lanterns and screens)

Green Farm Plants
Bury Court
Bentley
Farnham
Surrey GU10 5LZ
tel: 01420 23202
(hardy perennials, grasses)

Ken Muir Nurseries
Honeypot Farm
Rectory Road
Weeley Heath
Clacton-on-Sea
Essex CO16 9BJ
tel: 01255 830181
(fruit specialist)

Outdoor Lighting
Surrey Business Park
Weston Road
Epsom, Surrey KT17 1JG
tel: 01372 8488818
(full design and free advisory service)

The Palm Centre Ltd
Ham Central Nursery
Ham, Richmond
Surrey TW10 7HA
tel: 020 8255 6191
(palms, cycads, giant ferns)

Pots and Pithoi
The Barns, East Street
Turners Hill
Crawley
West Sussex RH10 4QQ
tel: 01342 714793
(Cretan terracotta and Mediterranean antique pots)

Rowden Gardens
Rowden, Brentor
Tavistock
Devon PL19 0NG
tel: 01822 810275
(rare and unusual water plants)

Royal Horticultural Society
80 Vincent Square
London SW1P 2PF
tel: 020 7834 4333
(advice, publications and details of RHS garden shows)

Rusco Marketing
Little Faringdon Mill
Lechlade
Gloucestershire GL7 3QQ
tel: 01367 252754
(extensive range of furniture, pots and parasols)

Tendercare Nurseries Ltd
18 Southlands Road
Denham, Uxbridge
Middlesex UB9 4HD
tel: 01895 835544
(mature shrubs and trees)

Vivid Space Design
699 Havelock Terrace Arches
London SW8 4AP
tel: 020 7498 9001
(versatile group of makers designing for gardens)

Whichford Pottery
Whichford
Shipston-on-Stour
Warwickshire CV36 5PG
tel: 01608 684416
(classic English, traditional and contemporary pots)

FLOORS & WALLS

PAINTED BRICK WALL

Dulux – ICI Paints
Wexham Road
Slough
Berkshire SL2 5DS
tel: 01753 550555
website: www.dulux.com
(exterior; masonry; paint)

Farrow & Ball Ltd
33 Uddens Trading Estate
Wimborne
Dorset BH21 7NL
tel: 01202 876141
website: www.farrow-ball.com
(exterior; masonry; paint)

Jungle Giants
Burford House Gardens
Tenbury Wells
Worcestershire WR15 8HQ
tel: 01584 819885
(bamboo, grasses)

P W Plants
Sunnyside
Heath Road, Kenninghall
Norwich, Norfolk NR16 2DS
tel: 01953 888212
(bamboo, grasses)

SLATE WITH TIMBER STEPPING STONES

Akzo Nobel Woodcare
Meadow Lane, St Ives
Huntingdon
Cambridgeshire PE17 4UY
tel: 01480 496868
(exterior paints and stains)

Civil Engineering Developments
728 London Road
West Thurrock
Grays
Essex RM20 3LU
tel: 01708 867237
(slate paddlestones; telephone for nationwide branches)

Langley Boxwood Nursery
Rake
Liss
Hampshire GU33 7JL
tel: 01730 894467
(box, topiary)

The Outdoor Deck Company
Mortimer House
46 Sheen Lane
London SW14 8LP
tel: 020 8876 8464
(bespoke timber decking)

The Romantic Garden Nursery
The Street, Swannington
Norwich
Norfolk NR9 5NW
tel: 01603 261488
(box, topiary)

Silverland Stone Ltd
Holloway Hill
Lyne
Chertsey
Surrey KT16 0AE
tel: 01932 569277

FURNITURE & FURNISHINGS

CHAIR COVERS

The Direct Foam Supply Company
13 Hillbury Road
Whyteleafe
Surrey CR3 0ER
tel: 020 8763 0424
(foam, latex)

DMG Antiques Fairs Ltd
34 Market Place
Newark
Nottinghamshire NG24 1DJ
tel: 01636 702326
(for nation-wide garden antiques fairs)

The Furniture Union
65a Hopton Street
London SE1 9LR
tel: 020 7928 5155
(modern cafe chairs, tables)

Habitat
branches nation-wide
0845 60 10 740
(contemporary metal and timber outdoor furniture)

Malabar Cotton Company
31–33 South Bank Business Centre
Ponton Road
London SW8 5BL
tel: 020 7501 4200
(cotton plains, stripes, checks)

Southern Foam
Dial Post Park
Horsham Road
Rusper
West Sussex RH12 4QX
tel: 01293 871875
(foam, latex)

Viaduct Furniture Ltd
1–10 Summers Street
London EC1R 5BD
tel: 020 7278 8456
(modern café chairs, tables)

TILED TRAY TABLE

IKEA
2 Drury Way
North Circular Road
London NW10 0TH
tel: 020 8208 5600
(lightweight, transportable furniture)

The Reject Tile Shop
178 Wandsworth Bridge Road
London SW6 2UQ
tel: 020 7731 6098
(wide selection of reject tiles)

HESSIAN CUSHIONS

Dylon International
Worsley Bridge Road
Lower Sydenham
London SE26 5HD
tel: 020 8663 4801
website: www.dylon.co.uk
(hand and washing machine dyes; telephone for advice and stockists)

Russell & Chapple
68 Drury Lane
London WC2B 5SP
tel: 020 7836 7521
(hessian, sacking, artists' canvas)

FEATURES & FOCAL POINTS

PAINTED BIRD BOX

Auro Organic Paint Supplies
Unit 1 Goldstones Farm
Ashdon
Saffron Walden
Essex CB10 2LZ
tel: 01799 584888
(natural paints, varnishes, stains)

LASSCo
St Michael's Church
Mark Street
London EC2A 4ER
tel: 020 7739 0448
website: www.lassco.co.uk
(architectural antiques, reclaimed materials)

Salvo
18 Ford Village
Berwick-upon-Tweed
Northumberland TD15 2QG
tel: 01890 820333
(list of regional dealers of antique garden ornaments and reclaimed materials)

RUSTIC MIRROR

See references for reclaimed timber in Painted Bird Box

Cuprinol
Adderwell Road, Frome
Somerset BA11 1NL
tel: 01373 465151
(timber protection and preservative products)

Liberon Waxes Ltd
Learoyd Road
Mountfield Industrial Estate
New Romney
Kent TN28 8XU
tel: 01797 367555
(specialist waxes, stains, varnishes)

LIGHTING

RECYCLED GLASS LANTERNS

The Chelsea Herbalist
PO BOX 4198
Worthing, West Sussex BN14 7HD
tel: 01903 210225
(bottle cutters)

Price's Patent Candle Company Ltd
110 York Road
London SW11 3RU
tel: 020 7228 3345
(candles, nightlights, outdoor lanterns)

SCENTED CHANDELIER

Avant Garden
The Studio, 3 Dartmouth Place
London W4 2RH
tel: 020 8994 0793

Chandelier Cleaning & Restoration Services
Gypsy Mead
Fyfield
Essex CM5 0RB
tel: 01277 899444
(old and new glass droplets)

The Conservatory Plant Line
Nayland Road
West Bergholt
Colchester
Essex CO6 3DH
tel: 01206 242533
(flowering conservatory plants by mail order)

Habitat
(see reference in Chair Covers section)

Noma Lites Ltd
Southey House
Vickers Drive
North Brooklands Industrial Park
Weybridge
Surrey KT13 0YU
tel: 01932 411330
(multi-string indoor and outdoor low-voltage lighting)

The Old Walled Garden
Oxenhoath
Hadlow
Tonbridge
Kent TN11 9SS
tel: 01732 810012
(conservatory plants)

Rayment Wirework Specialist
Laundry Road
Minster in Thanet
Kent CT12 4HL
tel: 01843 821628
(metal chandeliers, furniture)

Wilkinson plc
5 Catford Hill
London SE6 4NU
tel: 020 8314 1080
(old and new glass droplets)

WATER

CONTAINER POND

Chairworks
Units 77
Chelsea Bridge Business Centre
Queenstown Road
London SW8 4NE
tel: 020 7498 7611
(woven screens)

Ductaire Fabrications
Unit G
23 Grafton Road
West Croydon
Surrey CR0 3RP
tel: 020 8688 5188
(custom-made galvanised and zinc containers)

Lilies Water Gardens
Tarn Howles, Broad Lane
Dorking
Newdigate
Surrey RH5 5AT
tel: 01306 631064
(extensive range of aquatic and marginal water plants)

Oase UK
2 North Way
Walworth Industrial Estate
Andover
Hampshire SP10 3SF
tel: 01264 333225
(pumps, pond lighting)

Planned Environmental Services
Wealden Barn, Bethersden Road
Smarden
Kent TN27 8QF
tel: 01233 770795
(custom-made metal and galvanised containers)

BUBBLE FOUNTAIN

Beth Chatto Gardens
White Barn House
Clacton Road
Elmstead
Essex C07 7DB
tel: 01206 822007
(several varieties of gunnera)

Butyl Products
11 Radford Crescent
Billericay
Essex CM12 0DW
tel: 01277 653281
(specialists in pond and lake liners)

Civil Engineering Developments
(see reference in Slate with Timber Stepping Stones section)

Lotus Water Garden Products
Junction Street
Burnley
Lancashire BB12 0NA
tel: 01282 420771
(pumps for small water features)

Silverland Stone Ltd
(see reference in Slate with Timber Stepping Stones section)

Windmill Aggregates
Windmill Works
Aythorpe Roding, Dunmow
Essex CM6 1PQ
tel: 01279 876987
(specialist aggregates including aquatic gravel, grit, Crystaleis range of recycled crushed glass)

DECORATING WITH PLANTS

DECORATED POTS

Avant Garden
(see reference in Scented Chandelier section)

Border Hardcore & Rockery Stone
Buttington Quarry
Buttington
Welshpool
Powys SY21 8SZ
tel: 01938 570253
(suppliers of gravel and pebbles)

Cempak Ltd
Forge Lane
Thornhill Lees
Dewsbury
West Yorkshire WF12 9BU
tel: 01924 452644
(suppliers of pebbles, gravel)

Clifton Nurseries
5a Clifton Villas
Little Venice
London W9 2PH
tel: 0207 289 6851

Downderry Nursery
Pillar Box Lane
Hadlow
Tonbridge
Kent TN11 9SW
tel: 01732 810081
(specialist lavender grower)

Jane Hogben Terracotta
Grove House
East Common
Gerrards Cross
Buckinghamshire SL9 7AF
tel: 01753 882364

Hollington Nurseries
Woolton Hill
Newbury
Berkshire RG12 9XT
tel: 01636 253908
(aromatic herbs, scented plants)

Iden Croft Herbs
Frittenden Road
Staplehurst
Kent TN12 0DH
tel: 01580 891432
(aromatic herbs including lavender and rosemary)

Potmolen Paint
27 Woodcock Industrial Estate
Warminster
Wiltshire BA12 9DX
tel: 01985 213960
(specialist paint supplier including gilding materials)

Willow Pottery
Tog Hill House Farm
Hamswell
Nr Wick
Gloucestershire BS30 5RT
tel: 01225 891919

TWO-TIER CONTAINER

Avon Bulbs
Burnt House Farm
Middle Lambrook
South Petherton
Somerset TA13 5HE
tel: 01460 242177
(lily of the valley, smaller bulb specialist)

Burncoose Nurseries
Gwennap
Redruth
Cornwall TR16 6BJ
tel: 01209 861112
(shrubs, ornamental plants including hydrangea)

Ductaire Fabrications
(see reference in Container Pond section)

Fibrex Nurseries
Honeybourne Road
Pebworth
Warwickshire CV37 8XP
tel: 01789 720788
(ivy and fern specialist)

Fillan's Plants
Pound House Nursery
Buckland Monochorum
Yelverton
Devon PL20 7LJ
tel: 01822 855050
(hydrangea specialist)

Nutlin Nursery
Crowborough Road
Nutley
Uckfield
East Sussex TN22 3HU
tel: 01825 712670
(hydrangea specialist)

Planned Environmental Services
(see reference in Container Pond section)

Woodhams Landscape
Unit 3 McKay Trading Estate
Kensal Road
London W10 5BN
tel: 020 8964 9818
(galvanised containers)

RAISED BAMBOO BED

Akzo Nobel Woodcare
(see reference in Slate With Timber Stepping Stones)

The Cane Store
207 Blackstock Road
London N5 2LL
tel: 020 7354 4210
(bamboo canes)

Iden Croft Herbs
(see reference in Decorated Pots section)

Jungle Giants
(see reference in Painted Brick Wall section)

OUTDOOR EATING

SEVERAL IDEAS WITHIN OUTDOOR EATING

G Baldwin & Co
173 Walworth Road
London SE17 1RW
tel: 020 7703 5550
(saltpetre, culinary dried flowers, floral waters)

Norfolk Lavender Ltd
Caley Mill
Lynn Road
Heacham
Norfolk PE31 7JE
tel: 01485 572384
(dried lavender and plants)

Chase Organics
Riverdene Business Park
Molesey Road
Hersham
Surrey KT12 4RG
tel: 01932 253666
(organic seeds for flowers, herbs, vegetables)

INDEX

Page numbers in italics refer to illustrations.

INDEX

ACKNOWLEDGEMENTS

I would like to thank Linda Burgess for her inspirational pictures; Sue Storey for her sensitive design; and Emma Clegg and Liz Boyd at Conran Octopus for their support and enthusiasm. Many of the design projects in this book were recreated with the skills and expertise of Helen and Andrew Fickling, Steven Gott, Valerie Barrett, Geoffrey Love and Cally Law, as well as Frank Parr at Dylon, Rosemary Titterington at Iden Croft Herbs, Mike Wilderink and John Anderson at the Outdoor Deck Company, and Simon Harman and Hayley John at Lilies Water Gardens – my special thanks to you all.

The publisher would like to thank the following photographers and agencies for their kind permission to reproduce the photographs in this book.

2–3 Francesca Giovanelli; 4–5 Mirjam Bleeker/Taverne Agency and Frank Visser; 8 J C Mayer G Le Scanff/Festival des Jardins de Chaumont-Sur-Loire, France (Designers: E. Jalbert & A. Tardivon); 10–11 Anneke de Leeuw/Taverne Agency; 11 Marijke Heuff (Jardin De'Coursel, France); 12 Richard Bryant (Architect: Spencer Fung)/Arcaid; 12–13 Ross Honeysett; 14–15 Mirjam Bleeker/Taverne Agency and Frank Visser; 15 Gil Hanly (Designers: Ted Smyth and Ron Sang); 16 Winfried Heinz; 17 above Helen Fickling; 17 below Helen Fickling; 18 Garry Sarre (Designers: Stephan & Simon Rodrigues Stylist: Anne-Louise Willoughby) /Belle/Arcaid; 19 above Jerry Harpur (Designer: Fred Mengoni, NYC/Harpur Garden Library); 19 below Andrew Lawson (Designer: Dan Pearson); 20 Henk Dijkman; 21 Santi Caleca; 22–23 Melanie Eclare (Designers: Tindale Batstone); 24 Jerry Harpur (Designers: Jean-Marc Bourry, Marc Soucat, Chaumont Festival 1999)/Harpur Garden Library; 25 above Howard Sooley (Artist: Derek Jarman); 25 below J C Mayer - G Le Scanff/Festival des Jardins Chaumont sur Loire (Designer: Thomas Boog and Patrick Bailly); 26 Peter Anderson; 28 Verne Fotografie (A.Vereecke); 30 Mark Burgin/*Vogue Living*; 31 Helen Fickling (Designer: DeWet Loww, South Africa); 32 Beatrice Pichon-Clarisse(Designer: H. Peuvergne); 33 above Helen Fickling; 33 below Lanny Provo; 34 J C Mayer - G Le Scanff/Jardin des Paradis, Cordes su Ciel, France (Designers: E. Ossart & A. Maurieres); 34–35 Richard Bryant/Arcaid; 36 left Sunniva Harte (Designer: Goodman Portland); 36 right Andrew Lawson (Designer: Kate Collity); 37 Nicola Browne (Designer: Avant Gardener with Garden Design); 38 Melanie Eclare(Designers: Tindale Batstone); 38–39 Gil Hanly(Designer: Robin Curnaham); 39 Helen Fickling (Artist:Prinsloo)/The Interior Archive; 44 Marianne Majerus (Designer: Sarah Chrisp); 46 Undine Prohl (Architect: Ricardo Legorreta); 46–47 Marie Pierre Morel (Stylist: Christine Puech)/*Marie Claire Maison*; 48 Helen Fickling/The Interior Archive; 49 above Juliette Wade; 49 below Hannah Lewis/*Living Etc*/IPC Syndication; 50-51 Geoff Lung/*Belle Magazine*; 52 left J C Mayer - G Le Scanff/Festival des Jardins de Chaumont sur Loire, France(Designer: Eric Ossart); 52 right Helen Fickling; 53 Willem Rethmeier/*Vogue Living*; 60 Andrew Wood (Designer: Philip Hooper)/The Interior Archive; 62 Marijke Heuff (Designer: Mein Ruys); 63 Juliette Wade (Priory D'orsan, France); 64–65 Marijke Heuff (Jardin La Casella, France); 65 Andrew Lawson (Old Rectory, Sudborough, Northants); 66 Michele Lamontagne (Designer: Martha Schwartz); 67 Jerry Harpur (Designer: Nancy Heckler)/Harpur Garden Library; 68 above J C Mayer - G Le Scanff/Festival des Jardins de Chaumont sur Loire, France (Designers: C.Cheick-Gonzalez & I Ropelato); 68 below Georgia Glynn-Smith/The Garden Picture Library; 69 Helen Fickling (Artist: Prinsloo)/The Interior Archive; 76 Georgie Cole/*Vogue Entertaining & Travel;* 78 left Andrew Lawson (Designer: Ivan Hicks); 78 right Andrew Lawson; 79 Andrew Lawson; 80 above Guy Bouchet (Stylist: Bayle/Puech)/*Marie Claire Maison*; 80 below J C Mayer - G Le Scanff/Jardin des Paradis, Cordes sur Ciel, France (Designers: E. Ossart & A. Maurieres); 80–81 J C Mayer - G Le Scanff/Jardins des Fournials, France (Designers: E. Ossart & A. Maurierers); 82 Earl Carter (Architect: Andrew Nolan)/Belle/Arcaid; 83 above Nicola Browne (Designer: Martha Schwartz); 83 below Reiner Blunck (Architect: Martin Wagner); 92–93 Reiner Blunck (Architect: Glenn Murcutt); 93 above Alexandre Bailhache (Stylist: Anne-Marie Comte)/*Marie Claire Maison*; 93 below Winfried Heinz; 94 Andrew Lawson; 94–95 Jerry Harpur (Designer: Ken Ruzicka, NYC)/Harpur Garden Library; 96 Mise au Point/Chaumont 97; 96-97 Andrea Jones (Channel 4 Garden Doctors Series 99); 97 Melanie Eclare (Designers: Tindale Batstone); 104 Andrea Jones (Yves Saint Laurent Garden, Chelsea); 106 Marijke Heuff; 107 left Jerry Harpur (Designer: Jeff Mendoza)/Harpur Garden Library; 107 right J C Mayer - G Le Scanff/Festival des Jardins de Chaumont sur Loire (Designer: Eric Ossart); 108 Andrew Lawson; 108–109 J C Mayer - G Le Scanff/Festival des Jardins de Chaumont sur Loire (Designers: F di Carlo & M Sgandurra); 110 Marianne Majerus (Designer: Ruth Collier); 110–111 Henk Dijkman; 112 Marcus Harpur (Designer: Beth Chatto, Essex)/Harpur Garden Library; 113 above Nicola Browne (Designers: Avant Gardener with Garden Design); 113 below Jerry Harpur (Designer: Dan Pearson, London)/Harpur Garden Library (Designer: Dan Pearson); 122 James Merrell/*Homes & Gardens*/IPC Syndication; 124 Marie Pierre Morel/*Marie Claire Maison*; 124–125 Dexter Hodges (Stylist: Ino Coll)/La Casa de Marie Claire; 126–127 Martin Morrel/*Elle Decoration*; 128–129 Hotze Eisma/*Living*/VNU Syndication; 129 Simon Brown/The Interior Archive.

Every effort has been made to trace the copyright holders and we apologise in advance for any unintentional omission and would be pleased to insert the appropriate acknowledgement in any subsequent edition.